PROFILES IN MATHEMATICS

Women Mathematicians

Profiles in Mathematics:

Women Mathematicians

Padma Venkatraman

MORGAN REYNOLDS

PUBLISHING

Greensboro, North Carolina

Profiles in Mathematics:

Alan Turing

René Descartes

Carl Friedrich Gauss

Sophie Germain

Pierre de Fermat

Ancient Mathematicians

Women Mathematicians

PROFILES IN MATHEMATICS
WOMEN MATHEMATICIANS

Copyright © 2009 By Padma Venkatraman

Library of Congress Cataloging-in-Publication Data

Venkatraman, Padma.
    Women mathematicians / by Padma Venkatraman.
        p. cm. -- (Profiles in mathematics)
    Includes bibliographical references and index.
    ISBN-13: 978-1-59935-091-2
    ISBN-10: 1-59935-091-2
    1. Women mathematicians--Europe--Biography. 2. Mathematicians--
Europe--Biography. I. Title.
    QA28.V38 2008
    510.92'2--dc22
    [B]
                                    2008017056

28.95

Printed in the United States of America
First Edition

To Ambujam Karuna Lohmann, with love

Contents

Introduction

Mathematics gives us a powerful way to analyze and try to understand many of the things we observe around us, from the spread of epidemics and the orbit of planets, to grade point averages and the distance between cities. Mathematics also has been used to search for spiritual truth, as well as the more abstract question of what is knowledge itself.

Perhaps the most intriguing question about mathematics is where does it come from? Is it discovered, or is it invented? Does nature order the world by mathematical principles, and the mathematician's job is to uncover this underlying system? Or is mathematics created by mathematicians as developing cultures and technologies require it? This unanswerable question has intrigued mathematicians and scientists for thousands of years and is at the heart of this new series of biographies.

The development of mathematical knowledge has progressed, in fits and starts, for thousands of years. People from various areas and cultures have discovered new mathematical concepts and devised complex systems of algorithms and equations that have both practical and philosophical impact.

To learn more of the history of mathematics is to encounter some of the greatest minds in human history. Regardless of whether they were discoverers or inventors, these fascinating lives are filled with countless memorable stories—stories filled with the same tragedy, triumph, and persistence of genius as that of the world's great writers, artists, and musicians.

Knowledge of Pythagoras, René Descartes, Carl Friedrich Gauss, Sophie Germain, Alan Turing, and others will help to lift mathematics off the page and out of the calculator, and into the minds and imaginations of readers. As mathematics becomes more and more ingrained in our day-to-day lives, awakening students to its history becomes especially important.

Sharon F. Doorasamy
Editor in chief

Editorial Consultant

In his youth, Curt Gabrielson was inspired by reading the biographies of dozens of great mathematicians and scientists. "I was driven to learn math when I was young, because math is the language of physical science," says Curt, who named his dog Archimedes. "I now know also that it stands alone, beautiful and mysterious." He learned the more practical side of mathematics growing up on his family's hog farm in Missouri, designing and building structures, fixing electrical systems and machines, and planning for the yearly crops.

After earning a BS in physics from MIT and working at the San Francisco Exploratorium for several years, Curt spent two years in China teaching English, science, and math, and two years in Timor-Leste, one of the world's newest democracies, helping to create the first physics department at the country's National University, as well as a national teacher-training program. In 1997, he spearheaded the Watsonville Science Workshop in northern California, which has earned him recognition from the U.S. Congress, the California State Assembly, and the national Association of Mexican American educators. Mathematics instruction at the Workshop includes games, puzzles, geometric construction, and abacuses.

Curt Gabrielson is the author of several journal articles, as well as the book *Stomp Rockets, Catapults, and Kaleidoscopes: 30+ Amazing Science Projects You Can Build for Less than $1*.

Women Mathematicians: (from top left) Sonya Kovalevsky, Mary Somerville, Ada Lovelace, Emmy Noether, Emilie de Breteuil, and Maria Agnesi

one
Emilie de Breteuil,
Marquise du Chatele

Gabrielle-Emilie le Tonnelier de Breteuil, whose writing and mathematical work would help lay the foundation of modern mathematical physics, was born the daughter of a wealthy baron in Paris on December 17, 1706.

As a child, her parents considered her ugly, which, at a time when wealthy French women were expected to achieve little other than marry a wealthy gentleman, was a distinct disadvantage. Her father wrote that he would have prepared her for a religious life and let her hide in a convent, had it not been for the low opinion he held of several bishops. He described her as tall, strong as a woodcutter, clumsy beyond belief, with huge feet, enormous hands, skin as rough as a nutmeg grater, and altogether as ugly as a Gascon peasant recruit in the royal footguards.

Her father was so troubled by her clumsiness that he taught her horseback riding in the hope that it would help train her kinesthetic skills. He also got his daughter educated. This was unusual: the prevailing attitude among French nobility was that women had to be taught to entertain men in a frivolous manner. Intellectual females were seen as unattractive. Most European thinkers were also convinced that women were intellectually inferior to men and incapable of sophisticated abstract thought, particularly abstract mathematical and scientific thought.

Emilie's mother subscribed to the dogma of the times. Her advice to her children revolved around four tenets that she considered essential for a well-bred person to practice: (1) Don't blow your nose on your napkin, (2) Break your bread and do not cut it (3) Always smash an eggshell after you've eaten your egg so it doesn't roll off your plate, and (4) Never comb your hair in church. She had no interest in furthering Emilie's education.

Emilie showed early signs of a quick mind. She mastered Latin, Italian, and English, and by the age of fifteen, she had translated the *Aeneid* into French. Her greatest love, however, was mathematics.

Emilie surprised and delighted her parents by growing into a beautiful teenager, and by mastering the art of coquetry. When she was sixteen, she was sent to the French Royal court, and she began to use her mathematical abilities to win at gambling tables, a popular activity at that time. She used the money from her winnings to buy books and further her personal education. But beyond that practical purpose, Emilie continued to greatly enjoy gambling throughout her life. In an essay that she wrote later called "Discours sur le Bonheur" (Essays on Happiness), she expressed the view of an inveterate gambler, claiming that the only pleasures left to an old woman were study, gambling, and greed. She proclaimed that gambling for high stakes shook up the soul and kept it healthy. Flirtatious by nature, Emilie also enjoyed male attention and was never without a lover.

Emilie soon became engaged to Florent Claude, the Marquis du Chatalet, who was in his thirties. Emilie's parents approved of the match, and when Emilie was nineteen, the two were married. Within two years of the marriage, Emilie gave birth to two children—a son and a daughter. By the time she was twenty-seven, she had given birth to another son.

Florent Claude was a kind and indulgent husband. Throughout Emilie's life, he gave her the wealth and the freedom to live as she pleased. Although she was a socialite who enjoyed the frivolous pursuits of high society, Emilie continued to study mathematics and other subjects with passion. Florent Claude was happy to support Emilie's desire to be tutored by famous scientists and mathematicians. Interestingly, Emilie and Florent were content to spend most of their married life apart from one another. Though they always maintained a mutually agreeable friendship, Emilie had many extramarital affairs about which she was quite open, and none incited Florent Claude's jealousy. Similarly, most of Emilie's male lovers remained her friends long after they ceased to have a sexual relationship with her. One of Emilie's longest-standing affairs began when she was twenty-six. At the time, she met Francois Marie Arouet, who later adopted the name Voltaire. Voltaire was a noted writer and philosopher, and one of the key figures of the Enlightenment era. Voltaire was a fervent believer in the freedom of expression, and spoke out against the French monarchy and the Catholic Church, even when censorship laws made such talk

Emilie had a long-standing affair with Voltaire, a philosopher who was a key figure in the Enlightenment era. *(Library of Congress)*

punishable by imprisonment. Voltaire was nearly forty when he met Emilie, and on the verge of arrest. With her help, he evaded capture, and the two decided to live together at her husband's ancestral chateau at Cirey-sur-Blaise, which was a safe distance from the political hotbed of Paris, the French capital.

This love affair had a profound influence on Emilie and Voltaire. Their intellectual cooperation, which lasted from

Emilie's husband's ancestral chateau at Cirey-sur-Blaise (*Courtesy of Henry Beeker/Alamy*)

1733 until Emilie's death, sparked both of their minds. His entry in a competition sponsored by the French Academy of Sciences was instrumental in influencing Emilie to enter it on her own, and it was he who induced her to pursue what became one of her most important contributions to mathematics—a translation of Isaac Newton's *Principia Mathematica [Mathematical Principles]*.

Around 1734, Voltaire became interested in Newton's work, and he toyed with the idea of writing an account of Newton in collaboration with Emilie. Emilie was essential to the task: she spoke and understood Latin (the language Newton wrote in) better than Voltaire, and she was also far better at advanced mathematics—and an understanding of advanced mathematics was essential for anyone who sought to understand Newton's contributions completely. As a visitor to Emilie's estate at Cirey once observed, Emilie had such a quick mind that she once read out a text in French, hesitating just a moment at the end of each sentence. The visitor later realized that the text had been written in Latin, and that Emilie was translating it into French on the spot as she read it; the reason for her momentary hesitations was that she was working through the calculations on the pages as she read aloud.

When Voltaire suggested to Emilie that they undertake a study of Newton together, she agreed. They built a laboratory at Cirey, where they tested Newton's experiments (by repeating them) and explored procedures he had described. Emilie helped Voltaire understand the mathematics of Newton's ideas, by patiently showing him how to work through it step-by-step. Using her own insights (together with what she learned from their study of Newton) Emilie also pursued questions on her own: for instance, she worked out the pull of gravity on Saturn, estimated the amount of sunlight that would reach that planet, and how much smaller the sun would look if viewed from Saturn's horizon.

Together, Voltaire and Emilie completed a work on *The Elements of Newton*. Emilie was not listed as a coauthor; it was published under Voltaire's name alone. The unconventional couple had, for some reason, chosen to do this in accordance with the convention of the times (women weren't accorded coauthorship). Voltaire did, however, dedicate the work to Emilie, stating clearly, "the fruit of your worthy aid is what I now offer to the public."

In 1738, the French Academy of Sciences held a competition for the best scientific essay determining the nature of heat, light, and fire. Both Emilie and Voltaire were keen on investigating the question. They set up a home laboratory at Cirey and equipped it with air pumps, gigantic lenses, glass apparatus, tureens that could resist high levels of heat, and everything they could think of. Voltaire required Emilie's cooperation to help make the mathematical calculations involved in the experiments he designed. He suggested that they should try to measure every aspect of heating that was possible. They set small forest fires and measured the rate of a fire's growth. They had servants carry blocks of metal into forges in the forest near the Chateau, heat the blocks and then measure the weight; the results were inconclusive—some metals seemed to gain weight when they were heated, others appeared to gain none, and some actually lost weight.

Emilie supported Voltaire, standing by him as the experiments were performed and assisting with calculations. She quickly realized, though, that Voltaire was on the wrong path, and she decided to enter the competition on her own. She did this in secret, because she did not want him to feel offended that she was going against his scientific judgment.

However, because she and Voltaire were living together, Emilie couldn't perform experiments without his knowledge. Instead, she concentrated on the theoretical and mathematical aspects of the nature of light and heat. She began by pondering what she knew about light. From her earlier studies, she was well aware that light traveled at incredibly fast speeds. That, she reasoned, meant that if light was composed of solid particles, the particles in a ray of sunshine should hit the earth with such speed that they would shatter anything on the planet (like bullets fired from a gun). Furthermore, if light had weight, then shouldn't the sun, which was a source of light, be so heavy that its gravitational pull would be too great to let anything (including rays of sunshine) stream out of it? Perhaps, Emilie decided, light had no mass at all. This was a radical notion; most European scientists thought light had solid weight.

Emilie went on to wonder how light managed to heat up our entire planet if it had no particles or mass. She speculated that the heating power of light might come from the different colors in the light spectrum, and that there might even be more types of light than we could detect with our eyes. Perhaps, she suggested, there were solar systems beyond Earth, where suns glowed with colors different from that of our sun. We know today that Emilie's ideas were on the correct track—the electromagnetic spectrum includes portions that are invisible to the naked eye – ultraviolet and infrared rays, for example, as well as what is visible to us as light.

Emilie also hypothesized that if the colors in the light spectrum carried heat, each color must be associated with a different amount of heat. Emilie knew that to test her idea, she would have to use a prism, split the light into different colored rays and then measure the heat within each color of the spectrum using a thermometer. Unfortunately, however, she could not conduct this experiment without Voltaire's knowledge—because he had all the thermometers, and because if she did this experiment, she'd have to do it during the day. It would take time, and Voltaire would certainly discover what she was doing and realize that she had entered the competition on her own.

So instead of conducting the experiment, Emilie wrote up a report describing her ideas and suggesting experiments that could be carried out in the future. Emilie's idea was finally tested about seventy years later, by the scientist William Herschel. He split the light spectrum using a prism and placed thermometers within each color band. He discovered that some colors were cooler than others, and that even portions of the spectrum that appeared dark (or invisible to the eye) carried heat.

William Herschel

Emilie worked on her essay at night. All day, she helped Voltaire, who suspected nothing. To stay awake while she wrote, she would plunge her hand in a bowl of icy water. Although she was exhausted and severely sleep deprived, she managed to forge a substantial theoretical treatise.

Emilie was certain that her radical ideas, as well as the fact that she was a woman, would keep her from winning the grand prize, but she hoped that she would be taken seriously by the judges and distinguished from the crowd. Her wish came true.

In April 1738, the Academy announced the results of the competition. Neither Emilie's essay nor her cooperative effort with Voltaire (which was submitted under his name) won a prize, but both were honored with special commendations. Finally, it was made public that Emilie was the author of an entry. Maupertuis, a French scientist who had once been a lover of Emilie's and was still a good friend of hers, sent her essay to a noted English mathematician, remarking, "Its author is a young woman, of the highest merit, who has worked on science for several years now . . . she wrote it for the French Academy's prize—when you read it, you will find it hard to believe they gave the prize to anyone else."

Soon, Emilie's reputation as an excellent mathematician and scientist began to spread. Her next major opus was conceived as an essay on physics for her son, but it evolved into a textbook. *Institutions de Physique* (*Foundations of Physics*) was an example of Emilie's modern approach to writing: she provided definitions, historical background, and insights into the methods of thinking of various European physicists. She discussed the theories of scientists such as René Descartes, Christiaan Huygens, Johannes Kepler, Isaac Newton, and

Emilie discussed the theories of famous scientists like Johannes
Kepler (above) and Isaac Newton in her book *Institutions de Physique.*

Gottfried Liebniz. Emilie was evenhanded in her treatment of
various scientific modes of thought in her textbook; she sought
to help the reader understand the rationale and the achievements of each scientist, rather than trying to prejudice them
into following one person's views.

When the book was published in 1740, it met with great
acclaim. One of Emilie's prior tutors, Samuel Koenig, whom

Emilie had quarreled with a year earlier, declared that the work was merely a publication of lecture notes that he had shared with Emilie when he tutored her. She was furious, but by that time her reputation was well established, and most scientists and intellectuals accepted Emilie as the sole author of the work. She was further vindicated after her death, when Koenig was proven to be dishonest and unethical, having published a forged letter and other disputes.

Emilie's husband was proud of her scientific achievements, and became a very good friend of Voltaire's. Florent Claude sometimes visited the couple at Cirey, often going out on long rides with Voltaire. He also boasted to others about his wife's intellectual accomplishments.

Although Emilie's love affair with Voltaire was mutually beneficial and both of them achieved great heights of intellectual productivity while they were a couple, it slowly started to flounder. Voltaire began an affair with a younger woman, and Emilie began an affair with a younger man. However, as was typical of most relationships that Emilie established with her lovers, the two remained extremely close friends long after their sexual involvement ended.

Emilie's young lover was a courtier named Saint-Lambert. He was less infatuated with Emilie than she with him. At the age of forty-three, Emilie became pregnant with his child. Florent Claude came to Cirey to stay with Emilie to keep up the pretense that the child was his. Voltaire, still a most faithful and dear friend, came to keep her company and support her during the difficult pregnancy.

Throughout her pregnancy, which Emilie deeply feared she might not survive, she worked feverishly on an undertaking that Voltaire had suggested earlier, a translation of

Newton's *Principia Mathematica*. The translation of *Principia Mathematica* is considered one of Emilie's most important contributions to mathematics. This, together with her papers on fire, a manuscript on optics, and her physics textbook, had a tremendous impact on the advancement of French science. Emilie's work made a fundamental contribution to the advancement of mathematical science in Europe by helping to lay the foundations of modern mathematical physics, particularly mechanics.

Despite the difficult summer pregnancy, Emilie somehow managed to successfully finish the work. When Voltaire later described the birth of her child, he said the baby arrived while Emilie was working frantically at her desk, and that the newborn was placed on a mathematical volume when her mother finally retired to bed.

Voltaire, Florent Claude, and Saint-Lambert were all at Cirey, attending to Emilie's needs as she recovered from the birth, but she was unable to regain her strength. Late in the afternoon, on September 10, 1749, Emilie died. Voltaire, who was with her at the very end, was so distraught that he broke down and wept profusely. Ten years later, when Emilie's translation of the *Principia Mathematica* was published under her own name, Voltaire wrote the preface. In a poetic tribute to the memory of his beloved friend, he promised,

"I shall await you
quietly
In my meridian
in the fields of Cirey
Watching one star only
Watching my Emilie."

timeline

1706   Born December 12, in Paris, France.

1738   Given special commendation by French Academy of Sciences for best investigative essay on the nature of fire.

1740   *Institutions de physique* is published.

1748   Becomes pregnant with child of lover Saint-Lambert.

1749   Dies a few days after childbirth, September 10.

1759   Her translation of Newton's *Principia Mathematica* published posthumously with a *Preface historique* by Voltaire.

two
Maria Gaetana Agnesi

I n the summer of 1727, a young Italian girl, aged nine, addressed a distinguished audience of male academicians. "It will perhaps seem strange and unusual that I, not yet at the end of my childhood and having scarcely completed my youthful training in Latin, dare to speak in the presence of very distinguished men . . ." she began. "Clearly I should be afraid, lest they turn away from the purpose of today's oration, considering it nothing more than the frivolous opinion of a clever girl." The purpose of her oration was far from frivolous; it was entitled, "Academic Oration in which it is demonstrated that the studies of the liberal arts by the female sex are by no means inappropriate." She did not read from a script; she did not need to—she had a remarkable memory that she could rely on.

She went on to say there were three points that her adversaries often made against the education of women, and that she would "weaken and destroy them to such an extent that the deceit of empty gildings is removed and a plain and genuine version of the truth at last appears." She pointed out that they invoked custom and traditional views to keep women uneducated. Or, they suggested that the female sex was so weak that is was absolutely no match for the laborious study of letters and the difficult attainment of knowledge. The third argument centered on the notion that female minds should be "content with the management of domestic affairs, busying themselves with the needle and the spindle; these things and others of this kind, are proper to women, unlike pen and paper, since nothing is really more irritating than a learned woman in a debate."

In the course of her speech, the girl attacked each of the three points made by those who opposed women's education. She referred to them as unjust critics, enemies of letters and wisdom as much as of the human species. She said those who boldly denounced women, and refused to "bathe the tender minds of girls in the dew of knowledge," instead condemned them to "the eternal drought of ignorance," which led to barrenness and sterility.

She ended with an impassioned appeal:

"Thus, I ask this one last thing, very wise listeners, that you, who yourselves are defenders of letters and patrons in your judgment of our studies, and who always promote the advancement of the best abilities with your authority, might urge more effectively than I might assert with my voice, how adverse to the truth is the opinion of those who very stubbornly insist that the studies of the liberal arts are altogether unsuitable in women."

The eloquent, mature, and self-assured nine-year-old who made this address was Maria Gaetana Agnes, the eldest daughter of the liberal-minded Dom Pietro Agnesi Mariami. She was born in Milan, Italy, on May 6, 1718, into a wealthy family. Her father was a professor of mathematics at the University of Bologna, and he was proud of his children's abilities. He enjoyed parading their talents partly because he saw this as a way to ascend in rank. A social climber, he even changed the spelling of his family name to d'Agnesi, because this suggested that he was a member of the nobility. Maria's mother, Anna Brivia, was a refined and cultured woman. She also placed a high value on learning and took a keen interest in planning her daughters' education.

Maria was a remarkable child. At the age of five, a poet publicly praised Maria's remarkable fluency in French, in which she was as conversant as in her native Italian. By the age of nine, she had also mastered Latin, Greek, Hebrew, and many modern languages. It was probably after this that Maria began to study mathematics and philosophy, the subjects to which she would later make outstanding contributions. Over time, she studied and learned the mathematics of Isaac Newton, Gottfried Leibniz, Pierre de Fermat, René Descartes, Leonhard Euler, and brothers James and John Bernoulli. Two years after Maria made her speech, in 1729, it was reprinted in a volume entitled *Academic Discourses by Various Living Authors on the Education of Women, the Majority Recited in the Academy of the Ricovarti in Padua.* Only two females' perspectives on the question of women's education were included in the publication: one was young Maria's.

Maria's statements were stronger than that of the other female contributor. Maria stated boldly that women's education was necessary for the good of all humanity, condemned

As a child, Maria studied the works of famous mathematicians like the Bernoulli brothers. *(Courtesy of Mary Evans Picture Library/Alamy)*

ignorant men who kept women in a state of ignorance, maintained that a learned wife or daughter was an asset to a family, presented examples of erudite women that her father and her tutors had taught her about, and argued that women should not only be instructed by men, but also be able to instruct them. However, she stopped short of envisioning a place for women in politics, and clearly expressed her view that there were limits to what women would do with their education.

At the time, Italy was one of the few European nations where women actively participated in the academic world. For

centuries, prior even to the Renaissance, Italian women had earned doctorates and become lecturers and professors at the University of Bologna and the University of Pavia. Italian men were, in general, more broad-minded than their European contemporaries: as a rule, they did not stereotype or stigmatize strong women and considered intellectual women attractive. By the time Maria was fourteen, she was publicly debating mathematical concepts. Her father often invited intellectuals to their home and sometimes asked them to present seminars during their visits. He encouraged Maria to participate

Maria's knowledge of science, math, and philosophy impressed Charles de Brosses, a well-known French writer and politician. *(Courtesy of Visual Arts Library (London)/Alamy)*

in discussions with these distinguished visitors. One of the visitors, Charles De Brosses, the president of the parliament of Burgundy, France, was so impressed by Maria's questions that he wrote about her in his book *Lettres sur l'Italie* saying that she spoke wonderfully well on subjects as diverse as philosophy, human physiology, physics, and geometry, far surpassing his own knowledge on some of these topics. He commented on how remarkable it was to see a person of her age so conversant with abstruse subjects.

However, these displays of intelligence, of which her father was so proud, did not continue for long. Maria's deeply modest nature emerged, and when she entered her twenties, she persuaded her father to stop forcing her to speak with intellectuals. To her father's surprise and disappointment, she also asked his permission to enter a convent so that she could devote her life to her studies and spend the rest of her time working with the poor. Her father had hoped to further the family's social standing by encouraging his daughters to marry wealthy and powerful men. He denied her request, but Maria showed no interest in marriage and preferred to spend her time studying mathematics and caring for her younger siblings. After her mother's death, in 1732, she began to manage her father's household.

A few years later, in 1738, Maria published a collection of essays on scientific, mathematical, and philosophical concepts called *Propositiones philosophicae*. This was inspired by the learned discussions and debates that she had participated in, during the gatherings her father had organized publicly and in his home. By then, she had also started on what became her most important work, *Analytical Institutions*, a two-volume treatise on differential and integral calculus.

Calculus is a branch of mathematics that builds on algebra, geometry, and mathematical analysis. Calculus has widespread scientific and technological applications. The study of calculus focuses on changes such as curves and slopes. There are two major branches of calculus: differential calculus and integral calculus. Maria's work was built primarily on a mathematical foundation developed by the European mathematicians Newton and Leibniz.

Maria started *Analytical Institutions* for her own amusement, then she considered writing it up as a calculus textbook for her younger siblings. As the work continued to grow, however, it became clear to her that the effort would result in an important mathematical publication.

Maria was engrossed in writing the book for the monumental period of ten years. She began to pull together the work of various influential European mathematicians of the time, including Newton, Leibniz, and others. Her linguistic abilities allowed her to read the original papers written by mathematicians in foreign journals, instead of depending on translations written by someone else. She culled and collated what she considered to be the most important material she came across, after searching through a wide variety of sources.

Gathering together important methods and developments in the form of a compendium was only the first step in Maria's research. She also worked out several problems on her own so she could grasp the concepts she was learning, synthesize them, make insightful comments, and convey the information to the reader in a manner that would be easily accessible. Maria thought about her work constantly. At times, if she came across a problem that was hard to solve, she would go to bed, and arrive at the correct solution as she was sleeping. Immediately, she would get up and write down the solution.

In the first section of her book, Maria discussed topics in basic calculus, such as the elementary problems of maxima and minima, tangents, inflections, the construction of loci and conic sections, and the analysis of finite quantities.

In the second portion, she dealt with infinitesimal analysis. Infinitesimal analysis is a branch of mathematics that deals with "infinitely small quantities" (and sometimes also "infinitely large quantities"). An object too tiny for us to measure its length or mass or a tiny portion of time that is too quick for us to measure are examples of infinitely small quantities. In her text, Maria treated two types of infinitely small quantities as essentially the same: "differences" which are numbers that are very close to zero, but not zero; and "fluxions" which are finite rates of change.

The third section of Maria's *Analytical Institutions* is devoted to a branch of calculus known as integral calculus. Maria gave specific rules for integration, and also discussed the expression of a function as a power series, without referring to the extent of convergence. The final section of the book takes up two other areas of calculus, the fundamentals of differential equations and the inverse method of tangents.

In 1748, Maria published *Analytical Institutions*. It was immediately recognized as a classic textbook on calculus—the most comprehensive in the Western world since the publication of *Analyse des infiniment petits* (Analysis of the Infinitely Small) by L'Hopital, the first European book about differential calculus. Maria's book caused a sensation among European scholars; not only was it an incredibly significant piece of research, it was also the first major calculus textbook authored solely by a woman. It quickly became one of the most prevalent calculus texts in use at the time.

Maria's book was translated into French. A deputy from the French Academy of Sciences noted that he did not know of any work of this kind that was clearer, more methodical, or more comprehensive in mathematical sciences. He wrote to her that he admired particularly the art with which she brought under uniform methods the diverse conclusions scattered among the works of geometers and reached by methods entirely different. The high praise did not, however, result in Maria's nomination to the prestigious French Academy of Sciences. As was typical of the period, the institution barred women from membership.

Italian academics elected Maria to the Bologna Academy of Sciences. The Empress Maria Theresa, to whom Maria had dedicated the book, also honored her. She expressed her admiration by sending Maria a set of small boxes set with precious stones, and a dazzling diamond ring.

The recognition that pious Maria valued most dearly came from the Vatican. Pope Benedict XIV wrote letters to Maria in which he clearly indicated his profound respect for her exceptional mathematical abilities and dedication as a mathematical scholar. He sent her a crown set with precious jewels. He also urged the University of Bologna to appoint Maria as an honorary lecturer in mathematics.

In 1750, the Pope sent Maria a diploma stating that her name had been added to the faculty roll by the senate at the University of Bologna. Laura Bassi, a female physicist at the university, was one of many who encouraged Maria to take up her post. Maria served as the chair of Mathematics and Natural Philosophy at the University of Bologna between 1750

Empress Maria Theresa *(Courtesy of Visual Arts Library (London)/Alamy)*

and 1752, though her name remained on the university's faculty register until around 1796.

However, at the height of Maria's mathematical success, her father fell gravely ill. In 1752, he died, and after his death, Maria decided to give up the world of mathematics and academia. She began to devote her time and energy almost exclusively to charitable work. She became as passionate about caring for the poor in her parish of San Nazaro and the infirm

Pope Benedict XIV

at the hospital of Maggiore as she had once been about her mathematical research.

In 1762, the University of Turin wrote to ask her for her opinion of some recent articles on calculus written by a young scientist called Lagrange. Maria declined, saying that she had relinquished mathematics. Although Maria did not formally enter the convent (as she had desired to do when she was in her twenties), she pursued a selfless way of life. Showing little attachment to her worldly possessions, she sold the jewels given to her by the Empress and the Pope to raise money for the care of those who were old, ill, or poor. She even turned her own home into a place of refuge, looking after the needy in her own chambers when other facilities nearby ran out of space.

The energy she poured into these generous acts did not go unnoticed. The archbishop asked Maria to take charge of the women when the *Pio Instituto Trivulzio*, a home for the destitute, was opened in 1771. Maria accepted the responsibility, in addition to running the small care facility in her own home. Finally, in 1783, she relinquished her place of residence and moved into the Institute, but she insisted on paying rent for the rooms she occupied there, so that the Institute would be able to devote all its capital to serving the poor.

Maria poured her energy tirelessly into charitable work until she died at the age of eighty-one on January 9, 1799. Her death was recorded in the annals of the *Pio Instituto Trivulzio*, in which she was described as an angel of consolation to sick and dying women. According to her wishes, she was buried in a common grave with fifteen others, in a cemetery outside the Roman gates of the city.

A hundred years after her death, streets were named in her honor in her beloved Milan, as well as in the Italian cities of Monza and Masciago. A school in Milan bears her name, and many scholarships have been donated to poor girls in her honor.

In 1801, John Colson, a professor of mathematics at Cambridge University in England, translated Maria's work into English. While translating Maria's work on a versed sine curve (which is a special type of mathematical curve that is roughly S-shaped in form), the professor made a lasting mistake. Maria had described the sine curve by the term *versi-era*, which came from the Latin root *vertere*, meaning to turn. The word *versiera*, however, was similar to the Italian word *avversiera*, which meant wife of the devil. Colson mistranslated or misinterpreted Maria's word, using the word "witch" in his work. As such, many later authors writing in English referred to the pious Maria as "the witch of Agnesi."

Of all the famous female mathematicians whose lives are recorded in history, Maria probably led the most saintly lifestyle. Her religious nature and the extraordinary energy that she poured into charitable work are a testament to her angelic disposition. However, there is little doubt that she was, in the best and most complimentary sense of the word, a "witch" with numbers.

timeline

1718   Born in Milan on May 16.

1726   Gives oration in defense of a woman's right to education.

1729   Invited to contribute to publication on women's rights to education.

1732   Mother dies; begins to manage father's household.

1738   Publishes *Propositiones philosophicae*.

1748   Publishes *Instituzioni analitiche.*

1750-

1753   Occupies the position of Chair of Mathematics at the University of Bologna.

1752   Father dies; begins to spend more time on charitable causes.

1771   *Pio Instituto Trivulzio* opens; takes up an invitation to direct the women there.

1783   Takes up full-time residence at Pio Instituto Trivulzio.

1799   Dies January 9; in accordance with her wishes, is buried among the poor in a common grave.

1801   *Propositiones philosophicae* translated into English by John Colson.

three
Mary Somerville

By a curious coincidence, Mary Fairfax Somerville was born at the home of her cousin and future husband in Jedburgh, Scotland, on December 26, 1780. She came from a well established, though not especially well-to-do Fairfax family. Her mother, Margaret Charters, was the daughter of Samuel Charters, the solicitor of customs in Scotland, who was descended from a respected Scottish family. Her father, Admiral Sir William Fairfax, was George Washington's distant cousin. During the American Revolutionary War, George Washington sent Mary's father (then Lieutenant Fairfax) a letter referring to their relationship and inviting him to pay a visit. Mary's father, a British naval officer, declined the offer.

Admiral Fairfax was away at sea for long periods of time, and Mary's early years were spent largely under her mother's care, at her parents' home in the conservative community

A modern aerial view of Burntisland, Scotland, where Mary spent most of her early years. *(Courtesy of Malcolm Fife/Alamy)*

of Burntisland: "a small quiet seaport town with little or no commerce, situated on the coast of Fife, immediately opposite to Edinburgh . . . The manners and customs of the people who inhabited this pretty spot at the time were exceedingly primitive." Mary's carefree childhood included very little education. She later recalled: "My mother taught me to read the Bible, and to say my prayers morning and evening; otherwise she allowed me to grow up a wild creature." Mary spent most of her days outdoors, combing the beaches, admiring the flowers "which flourished luxuriantly on the front of the house" and watching birds. She "knew most of them, their flight and their habits." This carefree period ended abruptly, Mary recalled:

> [I] was between eight and nine years old, my father came home from sea, and was shocked to find me such a savage. I had not yet been taught to write, and though I amused myself reading . . . I read very badly, and with a strong Scotch accent . . . My father at last said to my mother,— "This kind of life will never do, Mary must at least know how to write and keep accounts." So at ten years old I was sent to a boarding-school.

Schooling was not mandatory for most children in Mary's time. Wealthy families often taught children reading and writing at home, and it was standard practice to hire a tutor for boys. Girls sometimes attended their brother's tutoring sessions, but they weren't expected to. Expectations of girls were few, as voiced by Mary's father: reading, writing, and keeping household accounts were "all that a woman was expected to know."

Mary was miserable at boarding school, where she had none of the freedom she had enjoyed at home. She wrote later that she felt shy, timid, and afraid of strangers, although her schoolmates were kind and often bathed her eyes to prevent her stern headmistress from seeing that Mary was perpetually in tears. The lessons she was taught also failed to inspire her:

> The chief thing I had to do was to learn by heart a page of Johnson's Dictionary: not only to spell the words, give their parts of speech, and meaning, but, as an exercise of memory, to remember their order of succession. Besides, I had to learn the first principles of writing, and the rudiments of French and English grammar. The method of teaching was extremely tedious and inefficient.

At the end of a year, Mary returned home, about as uneducated as when she had left. Her parents were dissatisfied and decided that the school was too expensive for Mary to return, given that she had learnt so little there. The decision was made to keep Mary at home for good, and ensure that a large part of her time was devoted to learning what was deemed useful for domestic life. After doing her duties each day, she was allowed to amuse herself in any way she wanted. Mary was as delighted at this change in affairs as "a wild animal escaped out of a cage." She did not have many companions of her own age, but she did not feel particularly lonely at her early lack of companionship; in fact, she enjoyed her solitude. She spent many hours wandering along the seashore, collecting shells, seaweeds, and seabirds' eggs; took long rambles on the coast and inland; "watched the crabs, live shells, jelly-fish, and various marine animals, all of which were objects of curiosity and amusement . . . and . . . soon learnt the trivial names of all the plants." When the weather was bad, she wrote that she did not know what to do with herself, until, fortunately, she discovered a "small collection of books, one of which was Shakespeare" and she began to read.

Mary's mother didn't prevent her from reading, although she considered it a waste of time for a girl. Unfortunately, however, an Aunt Janet remarked disparagingly that Mary did not sew more than if she were a man. This made her mother pay more attention to the development of Mary's sewing skills. At the time, housewives in Scotland were proud of their house linens. Families like Mary's grew flax on their estates, which their maids spun, but housewives devoted much of their own time to making and mending linen. Though Mary was annoyed that her "turn for reading was so much disapproved of, and thought it unjust that women should have been given a desire for knowledge if it were wrong to acquire it," she began to enjoy needlework, and Mary soon became an excellent seamstress. Mary's love for this domestic art remained with her throughout, and she left behind many fine specimens of her handiwork.

Although Mary learned to enjoy sewing, she still loved the acquisition of knowledge through reading books. Using the little French she had learned at school, she practiced French translation and taught herself history. Her mother allowed the village schoolmaster to teach her for a few weeks on winter evenings. He taught Latin and navigation, but these were not allowed for Mary, because she was a girl. Mary did successfully persuade him to teach her the use of terrestrial and celestial globes. She was especially fond of the latter, and "spent many hours, studying the stars by the aid of the celestial globe."

When she was thirteen, an uncle presented her with a piano, and Mary began to take music lessons. She enjoyed music enough to practice four or five hours a day, and rose early each morning to make sure she had enough time to practice. At first, she played so forcefully that she broke the strings. There was

Celestial Globe
(Courtesy of The London Art Archive/Alamy)

no piano tuner in her village, however, so Mary learned to mend the broken strings and tune the instrument on her own.

That same year, Mary spent the summer in Jedburgh, at the home of her uncle, Dr. Somerville, where she had been born. In her uncle, she met, for the first time in her life, a friend who approved of her thirst for knowledge. The two took many long walks together, and she became so close to him that she confessed she had been trying for a while to learn Latin on her own, and had not gotten very far. She was convinced that it was impossible for her to have much success at Latin because she was a girl. Dr. Somerville assured her, "on the contrary, that in ancient times many women—some of them of the highest rank in England—had been very elegant scholars." He began to tutor her in Latin.

Mary later said of this period, "I never was happier in my life than during the months I spent at Jedburgh. My aunt was a charming companion—witty, full of anecdote, and had read more than most women of her day." She found that her aunt's favorite author was Shakespeare, whose works Mary had read earlier.

The encouragement Mary received at the Somervilles' home had a deep impact on her, socially and academically. She became a friendly, out-going person, full of confidence. With newfound self assurance, Mary began to study many subjects on her own.

Mary's next family visit, to the house of the maternal uncle who had given her a piano, was not as wonderful as her visit with the Somervilles. "Though kind in the main, my uncle and his wife were rather sarcastic and severe, and kept me down a good deal, which I felt keenly, but said nothing. I was not a favorite . . . in consequence of the silence I was obliged to observe on the subjects which interested me." Despite their slightly severe disposition, Mary's aunt and uncle sent her to a dancing school. They also sent her to a school for writing and arithmetic, and Mary "made considerable progress in the latter, for I liked it." She also later remarked that she "could remember neither names or dates . . . yet . . . could play long pieces of music on the piano without the book, and never forget mathematical formulae."

Upon her return to her parents' home, Mary began to take a keen interest in politics. The French Revolution had just broken out. At first, according to Mary, there was general sympathy in Britain for the French revolt against their corrupt and tyrannical aristocracy, but the violent turn taken by the revolution made many people revert to a conservative stance. Those who supported the revolution were considered liberals. Mary's father was a conservative Tory, who opposed revolutions. An incident occurred which solidified Mary's political views. She recalled:

> The Liberals were distinguished by wearing their hair short, and when one day I happened to say how becoming a crop was, and that I wished the men would cut off those ugly pigtails, my father exclaimed, "By G_, when a man cuts off his queue, the head should go with it." The unjust and exaggerated abuse of the Liberal Party made me a Liberal. From my earliest years, my mind revolted against oppression and tyranny, and I resented the injustice of the world in denying all those privileges of education to my sex which were so lavishly bestowed on men. My liberal opinions, both in religion and politics, have remained unchanged (or rather, have advanced) throughout my life, but I have never been a republican. I have always considered a highly-educated aristocracy essential, not only for the government, but for the refinement of the people.

After her return home to Burntisland, Mary found that she was expected to accompany her mother to tea parties. At the age of about fifteen, at a tea party in her hometown, Mary and her friend Miss Ogilvie, bored by the company of older women, escaped into another room. As they perused a monthly ladies' magazine, Mary noticed that strange symbols were printed on one of the pages. As Mary's daughter later recorded, "Strange to say, she found . . . in an illustrated Magazine of Fashions, the introduction to the great study of her life." Mary recalled the incident in her autobiography:

> At the end of a page, I read what appeared to me to be simply an arithmetical question, but on turning the page I was surprised to see strange-looking lines mixed with letters, chiefly X's and Y's and asked; 'What is that?' 'Oh,' said Miss Ogilvie, 'it is a kind of arithmetic: they call it Algebra; but I can tell you nothing about it.' And we talked about other things; but on going home, I thought I would look if any of our books could tell me what was meant by algebra. In Robertson's 'Navigation' I flattered myself that I had got precisely what I wanted; but I soon found that I was mistaken. I perceived, however, that astronomy did not consist in star-gazing, and as I persevered in studying the book for a time, I certainly got a dim view of several subjects which were useful to me afterwards. Unfortunately, not one of our acquaintances or relations knew anything of science or natural history, nor, had they done so, should I have had courage to ask any of them a question, for I should have been laughed at. I was often very sad and forlorn; not a hand held out to help me.

The lack of any kind of familial support might have forced others to give up trying to study algebra; but not Mary. She later said, "I never lost sight of an object which had interested me."

In addition to attending parties and the theater (which she greatly enjoyed), Mary practiced music, kept up with her other studies, learned Greek on her own, helped with household work, made and mended her own clothes, and attended cooking lessons.

Mary also "took a fancy to learn to draw." Her mother was willing to encourage her in this pursuit, which was considered refined and feminine, and allowed Mary to attend an academy run by a reputed landscape artist called Nasmyth. Interestingly, this enabled her "to get elementary books on Algebra and Geometry without asking questions of any one," because Nasmyth, who regarded Mary the cleverest young lady he ever taught, encouraged his students to learn about perspective drawing. He told them, "You should study Euclid's *Elements of Geometry*; the foundation not only of perspective, but of astronomy and all mechanical science." At once, Mary realized that if necessary she could use drawing as an excuse to learn more about mathematics, though it was still impossible for a young girl to walk into a bookstore and ask for a major mathematical textbook.

A solution soon presented itself in the form of a man named Mr. Craw, who was hired to tutor Mary's brother Henry. Mary quickly befriended him, and requested that he purchase the math books she needed. Craw agreed, and even listened while Mary demonstrated a few problems for him.

Studying the advanced math books, Mary was initially discouraged when she realized she lacked the talent for basic addition. But she still understood more advanced mathematics, and yearned to know more. She stayed up late reading Euclid because she had to spend time on domestic tasks during the day. The servants complained to her mother about the diminishing supply of candles, saying, "It was no wonder the stock of candles was soon exhausted, for Miss Mary sat up reading till a very late hour; whereupon an order was given to take away Mary's candle, as soon as she was in bed." Mary had by this time, "already gone through the first six books of Euclid," and so she spent hours in the darkness "demonstrating in my mind a certain number of problems every night, till I could nearly go through the whole."

For a while, when Mary no longer had enough light in the evenings to work out problems on paper, she was content to continue with her mental mathematics, staying awake and working out problems from memory. Then, she decided that thinking through problems in her head was not enough. To devote more time to mathematics, she changed her schedule, rising early every morning to study in her bed before breakfast, wrapped in blankets.

As soon as her concentration waned, she rested her mind by switching to another task such as needlework or by reading a book of poetry or a novel. Mary loved novels, ghost stories in particular. These tales made quite an impression on her: when she was in her eighty-ninth year, she confessed that she did not sleep comfortably unless some one was nearby, and was especially afraid to sleep alone on stormy nights.

After reading a story or doing needlework for a while, when her mind felt fresh again, Mary returned to the mathematical problem she'd been working on. This, she felt, was the best way for her to work, by staying aware of her own energy level, and moving from one subject to another, instead of forcing herself to continue when she felt fatigued.

Although the perusal of her studies became Mary's chief object in life, she enjoyed mixing with people. She had many friends, and was often invited by them to dinner parties where there were games, music, and dancing. She was "fond of dancing, and never without partners, and often came home in bright daylight" after having spent most of the night at a social event. By this time, she was such an excellent seamstress that she made her own dresses for the balls she attended.

Mary's friends belonged to the upper strata of society, as she herself did, but they were not extremely affluent. When a painting of hers was praised very highly, a wealthy acquaintance tried to put Mary down by saying that it was good that Mary had a talent that could help her earn her keep. Mary related the incident later, saying "Had it been my lot to win my bread by painting . . . I should never have been ashamed of it . . . I was intensely ambitious to excel in something, for I felt it in my own breast that women were capable of taking a higher place in creation than that assigned to them in my early days, which was very low."

In 1804, at the age of twenty-four, Mary married Samuel Greig, a distant relation of her mother's family, and a commissioner of the Russian navy. When Mary later described this marriage, it was not in the happiest of terms. She wrote: "I was alone the whole of the day, so I continued my mathematical and other pursuits, but under great disadvantages; for although my husband did not prevent me from studying, I met with no sympathy whatever from him, as he had a very low opinion of the capacity of my sex, and had neither knowledge of nor interest in science of any kind." Within three years of the wedding, the couple had two sons, but although caring for two babies was time consuming, Mary did not give up her study. During this period, she managed to master enough

French to speak it well. Greig died in 1807, leaving Mary a fairly wealthy widow.

Mary returned to her father's home in Burntisland with her children. Soon after, her younger son died. In her recollections, she wrote little about her personal feelings during this period of her life, recording the births of her children as well as her bereavements merely with the dates of their occurrence. She later directed her daughter to suppress everything in her recollections which were of a personal nature. What was finally published relates mainly to her studies, the interesting people she met, and makes hardly any reference to her feelings, personal triumphs, and tragedies.

Mary diverted herself from the pain of losing her baby by delving into mathematics. She rose early and resumed her mathematical studies, exploring plane and spherical trigonometry, conic sections, and Fegusson's *Astronomy* and attempted to read Newton's *Principia Mathematica*. She also achieved her first public success when she solved a prize problem on Diophantine equations (a special category of algebraic equations), which she submitted to the editor of a popular mathematical journal. She was awarded a silver medal for this effort, and the editor advised her about a basic course of study she could undertake when she confided in him that she wanted to educate herself in mathematics.

Mary's mathematical knowledge grew tremendously over the next few years. Now that she had money of her own, she engaged a tutor to help with her studies—until she discovered that she knew more than he did. She studied calculus and became acquainted with a professor of mathematics at the University of Edinburgh. When she "told him that I earnestly desired to go through a regular course of

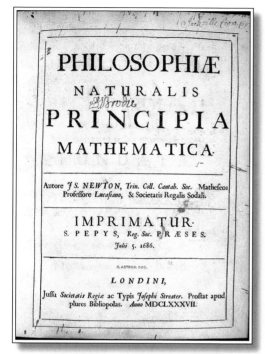

PHILOSOPHIÆ

N A T U R A L I S

P R I N C I P I A

M A T H E M A T I C A.

Autore JS. NEWTON, Trin. Coll. Cantab. Soc. Mathefeos Profeffore Lucafiano, & Societatis Regalis Sodali.

IMPRIMATUR·
S. P E P Y S, Reg. Soc. P R Æ S E S.
Julii 5. 1686.

R. ASTRON. SOC.

L O N D I N I,

Juffu Societatis Regiæ ac Typis Jofephi Streater. Proftat apud plures Bibliopolas. Anno MDCLXXXVII.

After the death of Mary's younger son, she distracted herself by reading mathematical texts like Isaac Newton's *Principia Mathematica.* (*Courtesy of The Print Collector/Alamy*)

mathematical and astronomical science, even including the highest branches, he gave me a list of the requisite books." Mary, now thirty-three years old, bought all the books he recommended and began to create her own small personal library. This collection was, at her death, presented to the Women's College at Girton, Cambridge. Mary was delighted with her purchases:

> I could hardly believe that I possessed such a treasure when I looked back on the day that I first saw the mysterious word "Algebra," and the long course of years in which I had persevered, almost without hope. It taught me never to despair. I now pursued my studies with increased assiduity; concealment was no longer possible, nor was it attempted. I was considered eccentric and foolish, and my conduct was highly disapproved by many, especially by some members of my own family.

Not all Mary's family members were critical of her. One of her cousins, William Somerville, who was a surgeon in the British Navy, admired her greatly. He was the son of her uncle, Dr. Somerville, who had earlier encouraged Mary in the pursuit of knowledge. William fell in love with his widowed cousin and proposed marriage. The couple married in 1812.

William's parents were delighted by the match, but unfortunately William's siblings were displeased. They had decided that Mary was too intellectual. One of his younger sisters wrote to her, shortly after the wedding, saying she hoped Mary would now give up her "foolish manner of life and studies, and make a respectable and useful wife." Mary was indignant, and William "still more so. He wrote a severe and angry letter . . . none of the family dared to interfere again." But one of William's sisters, as well as William's brother and his wife, insisted on joining the couple during their honeymoon. His brother became ill, and he asked for some currant jelly. Mary observed: "my cookery was needed; I made some that was excellent, and I never can forget the astonishment expressed at my being able to be so useful."

The couple stayed briefly in London, where they had an active social life, and then moved to Edinburgh when William was appointed head of the Army Medical Department in Scotland. Unlike Mary's first husband, William was a devoted and extremely supportive spouse. He suggested subjects for Mary to pursue, and also encouraged Mary to interact with the tutor engaged for Woronzow Greig (Mary's son by her first marriage). Mary, though she was nursing a baby at the time, decided to follow William's suggestion to devote an hour of study each day to botany.

William and Mary had three daughters. Mary was actively involved in her children's education, and she also continued her own. She began every day by studying mathematics. She mastered mineralogy, and then paleontology, and geology, but she also made time for child rearing, housework, and social engagements.

Mary was happy in her second marriage. She and her husband loved one another deeply, and they led a cheerful life. William proudly acknowledged that she was his intellectual superior. He helped buy books that she needed, searched in libraries for references she wanted, and even copied manuscripts for her. The couple gained the acquaintance of many scientists and mathematicians: Georges Cuvier, a naturalist; George Pentland, a naturalist and explorer; the mathematicians Sir Charles Napier, Mr. Babbage, and Lady Ada Byron Lovelace; the astronomers Sir William Herschel and Caroline Herschel; Joseph Louis Gay-Lussac, a physicist and chemist; and Sir William Edward Parry, an astronomer.

Sir William Parry was so impressed with Mary that he named an island in the Arctic after her. One of Mary's friends, Dr. Wollaston, gave her the honor of being the first person with whom he shared one of his discoveries. On a visit to the Somerville home one day, he closed the windows of a room to allow only a narrow line of light to enter, he allowed the light to pass through a prism, and pointed out that seven dark lines crossed the solar spectrum. This incident was of great significance in Mary's life, as it spurred her to start experimenting on her own, rather than merely accumulating knowledge. Proud to be the first to witness this discovery, Mary began to investigate the phenomenon Dr. Wollaston had shown her, and she wrote her first major scientific paper.

Then, tragedy struck. The Somervilles lost their eldest daughter. Mary's *Recollections*, written many years later, provided a rare glimpse into the sorrow of her loss. In a letter

Sir William Parry, an explorer, named an island in the Arctic after Mary. *(Courtesy of Hulton Archive/Getty Images)*

dated October 1823, she wrote to her father-in-law, "I never was so long of writing to you, but when the heart is breaking it is impossible to find words adequate to its relief. We are in deep affliction, for though the first violence of grief has subsided, there has succeeded a calm sorrow not less painful, a feeling of hopelessness in this world which only finds comfort in the prospect of another." Until this loss, Mary had been preoccupied with acquiring knowledge. After the loss of her daughter, however, Mary began to focus on sharing her knowledge with others.

The paper that Mary had written on her investigations into the solar spectrum was read before the Royal Society of London for the Improvement on Natural Knowledge in 1826. In this work, Mary tried to demonstrate that the violet rays in the solar spectrum had a magnetic influence. Later, her idea was proven untrue, and Mary felt ashamed of this early work. Although it was incorrect, however, it was a highly significant landmark in the history of science. It was one of the first papers authored solely by a woman to be presented to the Royal Society and to be published in their *Philosophical Transactions*. The interest aroused by her paper lead to several other important scientific investigations into the nature of light and the solar spectrum. Mary herself wrote a few more papers on the subject. Furthermore, the paper established her reputation, not merely as a person with an astonishing store of mathematical and scientific knowledge, but also as a scientific practitioner and independent researcher.

Mary continued her investigations into the solar spectrum for some years. In 1837, her second paper on the subject appeared in the *Edinburgh Philosophical Journal*'s twenty-second volume. It dealt with the transmission of rays of the solar spectrum through different media.

In 1837, a few months after Mary's paper was read to the Society, Lord Brougham, a prominent Englishman, wrote a letter to Mary's husband with a request that showed how highly he and other colleagues valued Mary's abilities. He asked William to persuade Mary to translate a work called

Pierre Simon de Laplace *(Courtesy of Mary Evans Picture Library/Alamy)*

La Mécanique Céleste, which had been written by a French scientist called Pierre Simon de Laplace. Lord Brougham was certain that this was an endeavor so difficult that unless she undertook it, no one else could. Lord Brougham was not exaggerating how hard it was to understand the book. The book was written in such a complicated fashion that Laplace himself was often forced to spend more than an hour trying to gather up the thread he had dropped whenever he took a short break from writing. The result was an important contribution, but one that was virtually inaccessible to all except the most highly educated and intelligent.

For a long time, astronomers had theorized that the solar system had originally been a nebulous gas, and that planets were simply portions of this gas which were now revolving around the sun. The sun was considered the largest portion of gas. Laplace had set out to prove mathematically that this theory was possible—in doing so, he had used advanced algebra, never bothering to simplify his mathematics using diagrams or figures. Mary had mastered the contents of the book, and despite her disparaging remarks about her poor French, she had even conversed with Laplace about the work, in French. Laplace commented that Mary was the only woman who understood his work.

In spite of this, Lord Brougham's letter surprised Mary. She felt diffident about her French language skills and her ability to make the work accessible to others in simple English. She also thought that her "self-acquired knowledge was so far inferior to that of men who had been educated in . . . universities that it would be the height of presumption to attempt to write on such a subject, or indeed any other." William encouraged her to take up the project, and Lord Brougham paid her a visit to persuade her as well. Finally, Mary consented, after insisting on two conditions: first, that the project should be kept secret; second, that if she failed, her manuscript should be fed to the fire.

Mary went to work writing and translated while minding her two little girls. While she worked, the girls practiced their music, learned their lessons, and even discussed their childhood problems with her; but somehow, Mary managed to concentrate on her work. When her daughters were grown, they reported that even when their mother was involved with this highly challenging task, she had never once lost her patience with them.

Mary set out to rework all of Laplace's problems. In addition, she explained all the subjects Laplace referred to or assumed his reader knew, and added her own illustrative material, diagrams, and figures. It was no easy process, and it took her nearly three full years. When her simplified and accessible English version of the work, *Mechanism of the Heavens*, was complete, she sent the manuscript to Lord Brougham. He was delighted.

The book was published in 1831, when Mary was fifty-one years old. It met with high praise. Mary was "astonished at the success . . . all reviews . . . were highly favourable." The mathematician Dr. Whewell remarked: "When Mrs. Somerville shows herself in the field which we mathematicians have been labouring in all our lives, and puts us to shame, she ought not to be surprised if we move off to other ground, and betake ourselves to poetry." Another eminent mathematician of the time, Professor Peacock, wrote that he "considered it to be a work of the greatest value and importance." The astronomer, Sir John Herschel said he had read her work "with the highest admiration" and that she would "leave behind a memorial of no common kind to posterity." The book became a required text for honor students at Cambridge University and was used as such until the next century.

Mary's work was far more than merely translation; she had transformed the book through the original commentaries she added and employed her unique mathematically creative abilities to illuminate the subject in a manner that Laplace had failed to do. The book demonstrated that Mary was not

John Herschel *(Courtesy of The Print Collector/Alamy)*

merely a scholar with a deep understanding of mathematics, but also one of the few who could grasp the most obscure intricacies of a subject and transform and translate it in a way that made it understandable to many people.

The Royal Society of London was so impressed with her work that the members voted unanimously to have Mary's bust placed in their Great Hall. She was elected an honorary member of the Bristol Philosophical Institution, of the Royal Academy at Dublin, and of the *Société de Physique et d'Histoire Naturelle* of Geneva. She was also given an annual pension by the king of England. A few years later, she was made a member of the Royal Italian Geographical Society and awarded their first gold medal ever.

People who had always doubted her, such as William's siblings, finally began to praise her. Although this made her happy, she was most pleased by her husband's genuine appreciation. She wrote: "the warmth with which Somerville entered into my success deeply affected me. Not one in ten thousand would have rejoiced at it as he did. But he was of a generous nature, far above jealousy, and he continued through life to take the kindest interest in all I did."

In spite of all the knowledge and success Mary acquired, she considered her education deficient, because in her opinion, she had not mastered French, Italian, or any other foreign language. She also felt that she lacked creativity, and that women were incapable of creative scientific and mathematical work. She was unable to perceive that her own life's work clearly contradicted this notion.

Despite her academic successes, Mary remained interested in typically female (for the era) pursuits such as cooking. When she visited British ships that were preparing for an expedition to find a north-west passage from the Atlantic to the Pacific, she presented a large quantity of orange marmalade to the officers. Upon their safe return, she was told that they had discovered an island, which they had named Somerville, in her honor.

Soon after the publication of the *Mechanism of the Heavens*, Mary's health took a turn for the worse, and she was advised to lie in bed until midday. She spent this time writing. In 1834, another of Mary's works was published: a volume called *The*

Connection of the Physical Sciences. When she wrote the book, she was clear about what constituted the physical sciences, but there was general confusion about what the term referred to. Mary included those sciences that treated the properties of matter and energy, and excluded chemistry and biology—her definitions and her classifications of physics into subdisciplines laid the basis for our current understanding of what the word "physics" means.

In the book, Mary concentrated on the latest explanations of various physical phenomena and sought to connect the various branches of physics. She also discussed and offered opinions about various theories and discoveries. To write the book, Mary had to familiarize herself with many new subject areas, but her mathematical acumen enabled her to master all the material she researched. She produced a book that reflected the state of European physics.

While writing the book, Mary grew closer to the astronomer Sir John Herschel, and she herself became interested in astronomy. In 1835, Mary was elected a member of the Royal Astronomical Society (along with Caroline Herschel, Sir John's aunt), becoming one of the first two women to receive this honor.

In her third major book, *Physical Geography,* Mary included the astronomy as well as the physics, geology, and biology of the earth from a geographical standpoint. Her aim was to discover quantitative mathematical connections and interrelationships, and to determine the fundamental principles that shaped land and explained the distribution of terrestrial and aquatic life. Mary included aspects of human geography in her book. She voiced her opinions in a manner that showed growing confidence in her own authority, and

Mary worried about publishing *Physical Geography* because Alexander von Humboldt had also written a book about geography, but he encouraged her to proceed.

supplemented her discussions with tables of data and foot-notes. Soon after she started this project, William's health began to fail. Around 1838, they moved to Italy, hoping he would recover in its warm climate. Here, too, the Somervilles made many friends, but though Mary spent her afternoons and evenings being social, she devoted her mornings to her work.

Physical Geography was an advanced work, and required years of hard work and study before it was completed. Mary was initially worried about publishing the work because Alexander von Humboldt had also written a book on physical geography. Her hesitation turned out to be unnecessary; Humboldt admired Mary and encouraged her to proceed. In 1848, when Mary was sixty-eight, the book was published. In recognition of this monumental work, she was awarded the Victoria Medal by Britain.

Mary kept in touch with her male colleagues after she and her husband moved to Italy. On one occasion, Sir John Herschel wrote to Mary, asking her to try out a powerful new telescope that an Italian colleague, DeVico, was using. Although Mary was the most qualified person to judge

DeVico's claims, women were not allowed to enter the monastery, the *Collegio Romano*, where the instrument was housed.

As she grew older, Mary became an ardent supporter of women's rights, signing many petitions that called for a woman's right to vote, and even headed one petition drive.

The discrimination Mary suffered as a woman opened her eyes to some degree to other causes as well. She refused to use sugar in her tea during the American Civil War, because sugar was a result of slave labor. Mary was, however, a product of her times. She believed that white people were more civilized than others, and referred to Africans as savages, though she was at least willing to openly acknowledge that slavery was evil.

Mary's love for animals did not abate with age, either. She tried to get an animal protection law passed in the Italian Parliament. She expressed her view that "We English cannot boast of humanity . . . so long as our sportsmen find pleasure in shooting down tame pigeons as they fly terrified out of a cage."

In 1860, when Mary was eighty, she was widowed for a second time. William, her longtime companion and ardent supporter, died in Florence after a three-day illness. His death caused her tremendous sorrow. Partly to distract herself from her grief, she fell into another task: she began to write a book called *Molecular and Microscopic Science.*

Five years after William's death, another blow struck— Mary's son, Woronzow Greig, died. Even after this, she continued to write her book, hoping to prevent herself from dwelling on her grief. In her recollections, she recorded her impression that at least she was old and would soon join her loved ones, and so the separation was only for a short time.

Mary's hearing deteriorated, but not her energy. She still wrote regularly every morning, from eight until twelve or one. When she was eighty-nine, *Molecular and Microscopic Science* was published. The book expressed Mary's conviction that the new frontiers of science were in the worlds of atoms, molecules and microbes, and she discussed the most recent advancements she was aware of in the fields of inorganic and organic chemistry, molecular physics, physiology, and microbiology.

In 1872, she wrote: "I am now in my 92nd year, still able to drive out for several hours; I am extremely deaf and my memory of ordinary events and especially of the names of people, is failing, but not for mathematical and scientific subjects. I am still able to read books on the higher algebra for four or five hours in the morning, and even to solve the problems. Sometimes I find them difficult, but my old obstinacy remains, for if I do not succeed to-day, I attack them again on the morrow."

Although her hearing failed, her eyesight remained keen and she continued to sew. Her mind remained sharp as ever. She ended her *Personal Recollections*, written during the last years of her life, with the observation that she had every reason to be thankful, because her intellect was still unimpaired and her daughters supported her tottering steps, and by incessant care and help, made the infirmities of age so light to her that she was perfectly happy.

Mary passed away peacefully, in sleep, on the morning of November 29, 1872. As her daughter recorded, "She always retained her habit of study, and . . . Mathematics delighted and amused her to the end."

Shortly after Mary's death, her name was commemorated by the establishment of Somerville Hall at Oxford University in England, where a Mary Somerville scholarship was instituted. Her remains rest in Naples, Italy.

timeline

1780   Born in Jedburgh, Scotland, on December 26.

1804   Marries Samuel Greig at the age of twenty-four.

1807   Greig dies.

1812   Marries cousin William Somerville; writes a silver-medal winning solution to a problem on Diophantine algebra.

1826   Presents paper to Royal Society entitled "The Magnetic Properties of the Violet Rays of the Solar Spectrum."

1831   The *Mechanisms of the Heavens*, her English translation of Laplace's *Mechanique Celeste,* published.

1834   *On the Connection of the Physical Sciences* published.

1835   Elected a member of the Royal Astronomical Society.

1837   Publishes a paper in the *Edinburgh Philosophical Journal (vol. 22)* on the transmission of rays of the solar spectrum through different media.

1838   Moves to Italy.

1848   Publishes *Physical Geography.*

1869   *Molecular and Microscopic Science* published; awarded gold medal by Royal Geographical Society.

1872   Dies in Naples at the age of ninety-two.

four
Ada Byron Lovelace

In the mid-nineteenth century, a woman called Augusta Ada Byron, countess of Lovelace, conceived the forerunner of the modern computer. She devoted considerable time to how this "Analytical Engine" would work, predicted that this invention would be able to repeat and loop and change course in midstream, and she wrote the first computer program ever. She further imagined that the Analytical Engine would one day evolve into a device that could even play music.

Born on December 10, 1815, Augusta Ada Byron was the daughter of British poet, George Gordon Noel, Lord Byron. Byron was as famous for his poetry as he was for his unpredictable, rakish character. His marriage to Ada's mother, Lady Byron (born Anne Isabella Millbank and called Annabella), was a case of attraction between opposite extremes. Lady Byron was a strict, prudish Victorian woman; Lord Byron was

Throughout her life, Ada maintained a complicated relationship with her mother, Lady Byron (above). *(Courtesy of Hulton Archive/Getty Images)*

a known libertine. During their honeymoon, Lady Byron suspected that her moody, temperamental husband was insane. When a doctor pronounced him mentally sound, Lady Byron declared that Byron was morally crazy. After just a year of life together, the marriage disintegrated irrevocably and the pair

Lord Byron, Ada's father *(Courtesy of Stock Montage/Getty Images)*

signed a separation agreement. Two months later, Byron left Britain, never to set eyes on his wife or daughter again.

In nineteenth-century England, it was considered scandalous for a woman of Lady Byron's rank to separate from her husband. Lady Byron took care to make sure that she and her daughter were not ostracized from society because of the short-lived marriage. She did her best to make sure her side of the story was publicized, so that she would be seen as an angelic woman who had been wronged by a deranged man.

Lady Byron was far from angelic, but she was an unusual woman—in her own way as enigmatic as her husband. On the one hand, she was autocratic, domineering, controlling, manipulative, and self-centered; on the other, she donated much of her time and money to charitable causes and was an intellectual who had broad-minded views on women's education.

She had a complicated relationship with her daughter Ada. She supported Ada by educating her well and caring for her financially, but she also did her best to suppress Ada's independent spirit. Her concern for Ada's well-being was marred by possessiveness, a feeling of moral superiority over others, and her fear that Ada would fall prey to what Lady Byron considered immoral influences (just as her husband had done). A year after their separation, Lady Byron took legal precautions to ensure that she had custody of her daughter, unusual at that time in England.

As a child, Ada lived in her grandparents' home while her mother traveled. She received a great deal of attention and love from her adoring grandparents, whose lives began to revolve around her, and she had a happy childhood. She also had a devoted and caring nurse. She saw little of her mother in her earliest years. As a result, when Lady Byron returned, she found that the girl preferred her nurse's company to her mother's. This made Lady Byron so jealous that she dismissed the nurse at once. Still, she continued to travel a great deal, professing that she had to do this for the sake of her health. Lady Byron left detailed rules about how her daughter was to be brought up.

After he left England, Lord Byron often wrote to his half-sister to ask about Ada, because Lady Byron refused to communicate with Byron directly (as advised by her lawyer). Lady Byron replied instead to his sister, and in that round about manner, Byron acquired news of Ada. Some biographers portray Byron as an uncaring father, but there is evidence to show that he was (at least occasionally) filled with deep regret at their separation. When Ada was one-year-old, he wrote the third part of a poem called *Childe Harold's Pilgrimage*, in which he expressed his longing to see his daughter, even referring to Ada by name.

Even as a child, Ada showed signs of a brilliant and imaginative mind. Lady Byron was delighted that her daughter was intelligent, but she wanted to curb her daughter's imagination. She feared that if she encouraged the little girl's creativity, she would grow up to be as restless and as lawless in spirit as her father. On the encouragement of her old mathematics tutor, Lady Byron decided that the best way to control Ada was to provide her with strong training in mathematics and science.

Ada was tutored at home from an early age. When she was five, she already knew the meaning of the words parallel, perpendicular, and horizontal, and could add up to six rows of numbers. By the time she was six, she had a rigorous timetable: mathematics, English, and music in the mornings, followed by geography, drawing, and French in the afternoon.

Ada also learned that going against her mother's wishes would result in serious repercussions. She was punished severely if she said or did something her mother disliked, and rewarded when she followed her mother's wishes. Her mother did not hesitate to lock her in dark closets if she misbehaved.

Lady Byron also disciplined Ada by forcing her to lie perfectly still for long periods of time, weighing Ada's fingers down with black bags if she dared to wriggle them instead of remaining completely immobile. Once, when Ada asked a question about her father, her mother became incredibly angry, and she refused to speak about Byron.

Lady Byron's possessive care for her daughter combined with a selfish disregard for her daughter's own wishes set the stage for a tumultuous mother-daughter relationship. At times, Ada strove to defy her mother, but her rebellions were never too great. Ada allowed her mother to interfere constantly with every aspect of her life, long after she became an adult. She appeared unable to sever the strange emotional dependence on her mother, and never really made a strong bid to rid herself of her mother's clutches.

When Ada was nearly seven, her beloved grandmother died. Lady Byron inherited her parents' title and entire estate, making her extremely wealthy. A year later, Ada experienced severe headaches for a time, which prevented her from reading, her favorite pastime. When Lord Byron heard of this he inquired anxiously after her health. Byron also asked for portraits of his daughter, and about her disposition, habits, studies, moral tendencies, and temper. He exclaimed that he hoped the gods had made her anything save poetical, as it was enough to have one such fool in the family.

On April 19, 1824, Byron died. On his desk was a letter that described his daughter. According to his valet, the last words on his lips were a lament that he had never been able to see Ada. Eight-year-old Ada was still unaware of much other than her father's name. Byron's body was returned to the family vault in England, but Lady Byron did not attend the funeral.

When Ada turned eleven, her mother decided to take her on a tour of the continent. They traveled together for two years. In 1828, upon their return, Lady Byron arranged for Ada to continue her education with excellent tutors. That year, Ada created a design for a flying machine. Far from being impressed with her daughter's inventiveness, this incident awoke renewed fear in Lady Byron that Ada would become like her father. She admonished her daughter for what she referred to as fanciful thoughts, and redoubled her efforts to keep Ada focused on mathematics. This was unsuccessful.

Soon, Ada was asking mathematical questions that her tutor could not answer. He tried to steer her to the safer ground of practical astronomy, but Ada had inherited stubbornness and determination from both her parents, and she refused to stop thinking about mathematical concepts that surpassed his knowledge. Even in 1829, after Ada came down with measles, and resulting complications left her too weak to walk, she continued her studies with unabated passion.

Lady Byron appealed to another physician, Dr. William Frend, to tutor Ada. Ada exchanged letters with Frend and later with his son, Augustus De Morgan, both of whom became her tutors. In her letters, Ada did not hesitate to ask her tutors questions. In 1834, she wrote to Dr. William Frend,

> I shall be very grateful if you will be kind enough for the first time you have a few spare moments, to write me a letter about rainbows. I am very much interested on the subject just now, but I cannot make out one thing at all, viz: why a rainbow always

appears to the spectator to be an arc of a circle? Why is it a curve at all, and why a circle rather than any other curve?

Ada sometimes followed her questions with self-effacing statements begging her tutors to forgive her for what she referred to as her ignorant questions. However, her self-deprecation was more a polite norm than a true characteristic. Ada retained her independent vision and did not subscribe to the old-fashioned views that Morgan and Frend had about algebra. She possessed confidence in herself and refused to be swayed by anyone else's ideas on a subject. She sought, instead, to fully understand each concept on her own and make her own mathematical interpretations and connections. She wrote that she did not consider that she knew a proposition until she could imagine to herself a figure in the air and go through the construction and demonstration without any book or assistance whatever.

At seventeen, Ada was presented to the king and queen during her coming out ball. A few weeks later, at a party, she met the inventor Charles Babbage. That meeting changed her life. Babbage had built a calculating machine in 1822, which he called the Difference Engine. It wasn't the first calculator: Blaise Pascal had built a primitive calculator that could execute the four arithmetic operations (addition, subtraction, multiplication, and division) in 1641, and Gottfried Leibniz had constructed a calculator in 1674.

Babbage's Difference Engine, which was on display at the party Ada attended, was an impressive array of gears, rods, wheels, and disks. It had three columns, each containing several rows of toothed metal disks inscribed on the rims with the numerals 0 to 9. The disks were stacked one

Charles Babbage *(Library of Congress)*

on top of another within each column. To add two numbers, each number was set on a column. Then, the two columns were connected with gears, and the crank was turned. As the crank turned, the teeth on the metal disks matched and meshed, and the columns turned until all the zeros lined up. The result of the sum was the number shown on the third column. Babbage's machine could also raise numbers to the

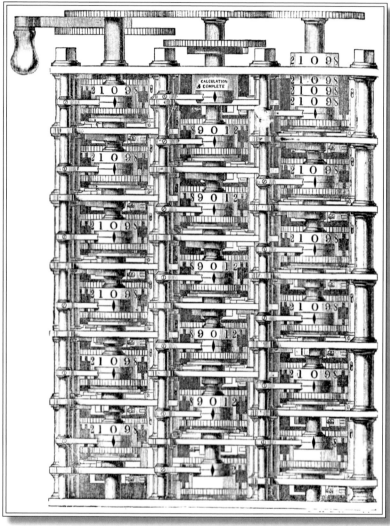

A diagram of Babbage's Difference Engine *(Courtesy of The Print Collector/Alamy)*

second and third powers and extract the root of a quadratic equation.

Most of Babbage's guests were content to marvel at the invention. Few of them cared about how it worked. Ada was different. The first time she saw the engine, she understood that the machine applied the method of finite differences. The method of finite differences involves computing differences (subtracting numbers) until there is a constant difference (meaning the next subtraction would produce zeroes). For example, the natural numbers 1, 2, 3, 4, and 5, when squared, yield 1, 4, 9, 16, and 25 (because $1^2=1\times1=1$, $2^2=2\times2=4$, $3^2=3\times3=9$, and so on). The differences between successive squares are 3, 5, 7, and 9 (because $4-1=3$, $9-4=5$, $16-9=7$, and $25-16=9$). If the next set of successive differences are computed (subtract pairs of the differences we obtained in the last step), 2 is the difference in every case (because $5-3=2$, $7-5=2$, and $9-7=2$). At this stage the answer is constant (the subtraction of successive differences has given 2 every time).

Obviously if the constants are subtracted from one another, the result is a series of zeroes (because $2-2=0$). Going backwards, adding differences will predict what the next number in the sequence will be. In this case, the constant was 2, so to find what the next number in the series will be after the number 9, add $9+2=11$. So the next number in the sequence 3, 5, 7, 9 is 11. Going one step further back, to find what the next squared number will be in the sequence 1, 4, 9, 16, 25, add the answer from the previous step (11) to the last square (25) and get $11+25=36$. The next number in the sequence 1, 4, 9, 16, 25 is, therefore, 36.

Babbage's machine used a broader version of this technique, and was capable of storing a series of numbers and performing additions with those numbers. Babbage understood that the general underlying principle of "differences" could be used to generate tables, computed through limited intervals, using one uniform process. He invented a machine that he could set up to comply with a law that governed a particular arithmetic series of numbers. Once it was set up correctly, the machinery turned to automatically generate the results.

Babbage was enthralled to find in Ada a beautiful young debutante who was brilliant enough to closely examine and almost immediately understand how his machine worked. He had received a gold medal from the Royal Astronomical Society for his invention and in 1823, the British government provided him with funding to build a larger model, which they hoped would generate accurate navigational tables to guide their naval vessels.

Unfortunately, Babbage underestimated the time and effort the project would consume, and fourteen years later, when the larger Difference Engine was nearly complete, he decided to abandon the project and start all over again to build a new machine called the Analytical Engine, which would stop as it was performing a series of operations, store the information it had, calculate what data it required for the next step, retrieve the stored information, and complete the problem by proceeding in this manner.

The British government, which had already spent an enormous amount of money on the Difference Engine, was aghast. A few people supported Babbage's bid to build a new machine, but most considered the project a waste, as Babbage had not even completed the first machine he had promised to build. Ada supported Babbage's proposal to build the Analytical Engine—the concept of this machine would draw their lives together.

One of Babbage's friends and correspondents, the eminent mathematician Mary Fairfax Somerville, met Ada in 1834. Soon, Mary Somerville had become Ada's favorite correspondent. Mary Somerville sent Ada books on mathematics, gave her guidance on a course of study, challenged her by sending her mathematical problems, and proved much more knowledgeable a mentor than Ada's other tutors. Mary also became Ada's favorite chaperone; Ada frequently accompanied Somerville and her daughters when they attended scientific and mathematical lectures.

Woronzow Greig, Somerville's son, became a close friend of Ada's as well. He introduced nineteen-year-old Ada to an aristocratic bachelor who was eleven years her senior, William, the eighth Baron King. As Woronzow had hoped, William fell madly in love with Ada, and the two became engaged. Lady Byron approved of the match. She felt that William would be a calming influence on Ada, and she went so far as to bequeath most of her wealth to William directly, so that Ada would only inherit it indirectly, through her husband. She ensured that Ada would have a pittance—three-hundred pounds per year—to spend as she wished. Ada resented her mother's control, but after a short engagement, on July 8, 1835, the young couple married at Lady Byron's residence.

Lady Byron interfered in the new couple's life as much as she could. Surprisingly, William, whose relationship with his own mother was fraught, became deeply devoted to his mother-in-law. Within a year of the wedding, Ada was pregnant with their first child. A son, born on May 12, 1936, was named Byron. Lady Byron hired nurse Grimes, who had been Ada's favorite nurse as a child, to look after her grandson. And on Ada's twenty-first birthday, Lady Byron sent her daughter a portrait of her father. A year and a half later, on September 22, 1837, Ada gave birth to a daughter who she named after her grandmother, Anne Isabella. The next year, on June 30, 1838, William took his seat at the House of Lords, as the first earl of Lovelace (a name he took from one of Ada's ancestors). Lady Byron was delighted. Ada was expecting again shortly thereafter, and on July 2, 1839, she gave birth to her last child, a son named Ralph, after Ada's beloved grandfather.

Ada and William were not the most devoted of parents. Although they made some loving references to their children, they also resented the intrusion on their time. William was, however, an adoring and indulgent husband. He shared Ada's love of horses, and the couple spent a great deal of time riding. William bought Ada a boat and built a harbor and a sea-water swimming pool because Ada enjoyed sailing and the water.

Ada and William engaged tutors for their children's education, but Ada was far keener on pursuing her own studies than in helping them with theirs. She wrote to Charles Babbage, hinting that he might tutor her, but he declined, offering other suggestions instead. In a few years, however, Ada and Babbage had become close friends and Ada invited Babbage to visit the Lovelace residence at Ockham Park in January 1841. That year, Lady Byron finally spoke to Ada at length about her father, painting his character in a dishonorable light. Ada did not adopt her mother's view of her father's nature, and her feelings toward the father she had not been allowed to know were tinged with nostalgia.

The year prior to his visit to the Lovelaces, Babbage had spent time at a scientists' meeting in Italy. There, he had presented his ideas for an Analytical Engine, hoping that an eminent scientist would be enthusiastic enough to endorse his plea to build such a machine. One of the Italians at the conference, a young engineer called Menabrea, who later became the prime minister of Italy, decided to write a paper in French, using Babbage's drawings and notes, explaining how Babbage's machine would work.

His article appeared in October 1842 in the journal *Biliotheque Universelle de Geneve.*

Charles Wheatstone, a British scientist, came across the article. He was a family friend of the Lovelaces and knowing Ada's aptitude for language and mathematics, he requested her to translate Menebrea's article into English and submit the translation to a British journal. Babbage, who had become an increasingly good friend of the Lovelaces, encouraged Ada, suggesting that she should write an entirely new article, rather than merely translate Menebrea's. Ada did both. Although she called her work a translation out of respect for Menebrea, it was far more than that. She added much new information, nearly tripling the length of the original paper, via what she referred to modestly as her "notes" on the Analytical Engine.

Writing the notes was not an easy process. Ada's health had been deteriorating, and her doctors prescribed substances that are now recognized as highly dangerous. She was encouraged to take opium and she took the drug with wine. As a result, Ada suffered mentally and physically. She had hallucinations, bouts of depression, and sudden bursts of frenetic energy. Her eyes burned, her body shivered, and at times her

Charles Wheatstone

fingers trembled so much that she could not hold her pen to write her manuscript.

Although her mind was suffering from the influence of drugs, Ada somehow was able to concentrate on her work and write the notes with astonishing clarity and insight. She expanded Menabrea's tables, created new ones based on her own calculations, and corrected Babbage's errors.

Ada's notes were intended to explain the working of the proposed Analytical Engine and also to garner support for the project. Altogether, she wrote seven lengthy notes, labeled with the first seven letters of the alphabet.

In the opening note, Ada compared the old Difference Engine to the proposed new Analytical Engine. She explained that the Analytical Engine "does not occupy common ground with mere 'calculating machines'" and that it was much more than an improvement on the Difference Engine—it was radically different in many ways.

One of the most important differences was that the Analytical Engine would use a technique similar to the punched cards used in silk-weaving looms. "We may say most aptly that the Analytical Engine weaves algebraical patterns just as the Jacquard-loom weaves flowers and leaves" wrote Ada as if the machine already existed (although the engine was still only in the planning stages). The Analytical Engine could thus be programmed to act on instructions, and it could pause and change those instructions mid-way through a process.

The Analytical Engine was designed to analyze data and give orders about how to proceed, as Ada clarified, it was "equally capable of analysis or of synthesis." The operation cards which instructed the machine on procedures were dependent on the programmer; it was the programmer who originated a sequence and provided the machine with a procedure. Then again, all the programmer had to do was to make sure the operation cards were correct; after that, the Analytical Engine would take care of the process.

The Difference Engine, on the other hand, required more human intervention. The operator had to perform computations and set calculated data on the columns before it could work, a level of preprocessing which the Analytical Engine did not require.

The Analytical Engine was designed to break a complex problem down into a series of smaller operations, like the modern-day computer. Ada pointed out that the Analytical Engine could further mathematical thinking because it would force its operators to think clearly about the logical procedures they used in any rational process. The Analytical Engine mechanically separated processes, data, and numerical results, forcing mathematicians to refine and clarify their thought processes as well as notations. They would be forced to separate symbols used to signify operations from those representing quantities, for instance. In this manner, Ada anticipated the idea of Artificial Intelligence—a machine that could mimic the human mind and simulate cognition.

In Note A, Ada also anticipated computer generated music. "Supposing, for instance, that the fundamental relations of pitched sounds in the science of harmony and of musical composition were" expressed abstractly and adapted to a notation that could be entered into the mechanism of the engine, it "might compose elaborate scientific pieces of music of any degree of complexity or extent" she wrote. In Note B, Ada took great pains to differentiate between the cards that determined operations for the calculations versus those cards that distributed the operations and separated them according to function. She explained the engine's ability to store intermediate results as well as final calculations. A theme she began in Note A, about how the Analytical Engine could further refine mathematical thinking was also reiterated in Note B: "The further we analyse the manner in which such an engine performs its processes and attains its results, the more we perceive how distinctly it places in a true and just light the mutual relations and connexion of the various mathematical analysis, how clearly it separates those things which are in reality distinct and independent, and unites those which are mutually dependent."

Note C is the shortest note. It includes a section on what Babbage and Ada called "backing;" a particular card or set of cards was used iteratively (in succession a number of times) to help solve a particular problem. Ada explained that "a method was devised of what was technically designated backing the cards in certain groups according to certain laws. The object of this extension is to secure the possibility of bringing any particular card or set of cards into use any number of times successively in the solution of one problem." Backing was also like a subroutine, a separate but related section of code that was pulled in for a particular program.

Note D provides an in-depth explanation of tables showing the functions of three kinds of variable columns—the first kind would hold data, the second kind would hold temporary information that was necessary for later use, and the third would hold the final results. Menebrea had only shown the first two kinds of tables. Ada added the third, noting that together, the tables formed a complete and accurate method of registering every step and sequence in all calculations performed by the engine. Several sets of operations could proceed simultaneously, so that independent but related work could occur at the same time. She reminded the reader that sometimes, several sequences could be used to solve a particular problem. The goal was to find that sequence which would take the shortest amount of time.

Note E demonstrates how the Analytical Engine may work through a problem. Ada chose to illustrate the algebraic as well as arithmetic power of the Analytical Engine by using trigonometric functions as an example. Many characteristics of this proposed machine resembled today's computers. Stacks of punched cards worked the way modern function keys do. The machine could also respond conditionally to instructions (similar to statements used in today's computer programs) to help it get through the steps of a procedure successfully. Ada explained, "whenever a general term exists, there will be a recurring group of operations."

Note F reminds the reader of a very important simplification which was a hallmark of the Analytical Engine that she had referred to earlier in Note C. It could use just a few cards to weave symmetric patterns. In Note F, Ada gave an example of how with just three operating cards, the engine could go through 330 operations. Just three cards could potentially be enough for doing millions of simple equations, she suggested. She dwells on the idea that the Analytical Engine will be able to solve tedious and difficult problems speedily and accurately. It could, she points out, compute astronomical tables without the errors to which they are prone when human beings have to do all the computations on their own. She also speculated that the Analytical Engine could be used to find new problems or generate sequences for mathematical amusement, just as today's computers can.

In her final note, Ada summarizes the main features of the engine and also warns that "The Analytical Engine has no pretensions whatever to originate anything. It can do whatever we know how to order it to perform. It can follow analysis; but it has no power of anticipating any analytical relations or truths. Its province is to assist us in making available what we are already acquainted with." She also predicts that the Engine would probably exert an "indirect and reciprocal influence on science itself" because scientific, mathematical, or any other procedures designed for the machine would have to be carefully analyzed and logically examined.

The note ends with a rather complicated example of the Engine's powers: a detailed account of how the engine could compute the powers of Bernoulli numbers. Bernoulli numbers are irregular and constitute a sequence that rapidly increases. Ada chose them purposely because they were a complex example, which could illustrate how the engine could on its own, perform calculations that had not been done by human beings, and in a manner surpassing those done by human beings.

During the course of her work, Ada wrote frequently to Babbage. As they drew closer, she often referred to him informally as "Dear Babbage" instead of using the formal Victorian salutation, "My dear Mr. Babbage." She did not hold back from writing rudely to him at times, when she felt annoyed. She often praised her own work, using superlatives to describe her abilities, telling him she was working very hard for him. If he dared to make edits that she disagreed with and on the occasions when she caught errors in his work, she criticized him severely. Babbage usually replied praising her writing greatly, but by the time the paper was ready for publication, their relationship had undergone a fairly strenuous ordeal. They remained friends, but they never collaborated on a project again.

Ada's notes were not only mathematically impressive, they surpassed even Babbage's own understanding of what his Analytical Engine was capable of doing. Her paper was published in *Taylor's Scientific Memoirs* in August 1843. Aristocratic Victorian women considered it beneath their station to write papers, and so Ada's notes were published under her initials, A. A. L., rather than her name. Although Ada did not sign the publication with her name and opted to adhere to convention by keeping her identity a secret, she was proud of her achievement. She purchased 250 copies of her notes and sent them to friends and prominent personages. Her work was widely acclaimed, but to her disappointment and Babbage's, it did not succeed in convincing the British government to fund the project. They wrote to Babbage soon after the publication of Ada's work to let him know that they would not give him the financial backing necessary to turn the dream of an Analytical Engine into a reality. Babbage was incredibly disappointed.

Ada was also disappointed; not even her academic success provided her with a sense of fulfillment. She was still operating under the influence of narcotic medications and the letters she wrote sometimes expressed a passionate ecstasy and boastfulness reminiscent of her father's character; at other times, she sounded intensely discontented. In 1844, she wrote to her mother, referring to herself immodestly as "the Deborah, the Elijah of Science" and as a mathematical

"Prophetess . . . However intensely I may love certain mortals, there is One whom I must ever love and adore a million fold as intensely; the great All Knowing Integral!"

Around 1845, Ada began to confide her increasing dissatisfaction with domestic life to her friend Woronzow Greig. She wrote to him saying that her children gave her little pleasure. She complained that she felt her marriage was lifeless, although she described William as a good and just man, and clarified that this was no fault of his. She also confessed to Woronzow that her ideas of matrimony and of the matrimonial institution were peculiar, and that no man would suit her as a husband. She said she was a fairy who didn't want a mortal husband. She did not write that she was having an extra-marital affair, but there were many rumors that she was unfaithful to her husband and that she had an affair with a man named Crosse, and maybe other men as well.

Ada began gambling and betting on horses. Her interest in betting may have begun as a purely academic pursuit. She certainly spent a great deal of time exploring the mathematics of probability and chance, and at one point, she and Babbage were confident they had devised a fail-safe betting system that could beat the odds. Babbage soon realized that this was untrue, and he stopped gambling; Ada continued. It seemed as though she had turned into a compulsive gambler, addicted to betting. She tried to keep this unhappy pastime a secret from her husband, but as she fell deeper and deeper into debt, she was forced to tell him the truth.

Although William had sometimes accompanied his wife to the racetrack, he had no idea of how deeply entangled Ada was. He was shocked by his wife's gambling debts, but he stood by her nonetheless. He promised to pay off her debts

In the summer of 1850, Ada visited and fell in love with Newstead Abbey, Lord Byron's ancestral home. *(Library of Congress)*

and the couple tried to keep Ada's habit a secret from her unforgiving mother. In the summer of 1850, William took Ada on a long holiday. They visited many old homes, including Newstead Abbey, where many of Lord Byron's ancestors had lived. Ada wrote to her mother that she loved the venerable old place and all her wicked forefathers. Lady Byron was furious.

About a year later, Ada was diagnosed with cervical cancer, and William confided this to his mother-in-law. Unfortunately, he also revealed the secret of Ada's gambling. Lady Byron was livid and blamed William for Ada's gambling habit. She sent a lawyer to visit Ada in 1852. Ada listed her unpaid debts and the lawyer reported this to Lady Byron. Lady Byron settled the debts, and Ada wrote to thank her, but their relationship grew rockier than ever. Ada was frightened to face her mother, and she wrote begging her mother to stay away. In August, 1852, she wrote frantically to Babbage, entreating him to act as her executor in the event that she died suddenly before completing a will. She gave him instructions on what to do and wrote how fully she relied and trusted him to carry out her directions, signing off with affection.

Lady Byron moved in with the Lovelaces during Ada's final weeks of life and cut off Ada's support system. She refused to let any of Ada's friends visit her, and dismissed all the household servants. She did not even let Babbage see Ada again. Instead, she brought over some of her own friends, who visited Ada to sermonize about how immoral Ada was.

William was so desperate to comfort his wife that he allowed Lady Byron to order him about. Lady Byron did not forbid William from seeing his wife, but she continued to blame him for Ada's condition. Although Ada was in excruciating pain, Lady Byron also insisted that Ada not be given any painkillers. She said that Ada must suffer pain in order to cleanse her soul of her sins and that the distress Ada was suffering was inflicted upon her by God as a necessary punishment for the salvation of her soul. Ada's children visited her sick bed, and her daughter looked after her with devotion, but Ada was in physical and mental agony.

At Lady Byron's insistence, Ada confessed her "sins" to William. This supposedly included an admission of extramarital affairs, although at least part of the admission might have been no more than rambling brought on by pain and drugs. Regardless of how much truth there was in her confession, the trusting William had never suspected his wife of having affairs, and he was deeply wounded. Finally, after much suffering and torment, Ada died on November 27, 1852, at the age of thirty-six.

Lady Byron, whose final actions toward her daughter had been so controlling, did not bother to attend the funeral. She did, however, do her best to go against Ada's last wishes. Ada had nominated Babbage to be the executor of her will, and had bequeathed her books to Babbage, but Lady Byron disregarded and disrespected her daughter's final requests. She ordered Babbage to return all Ada's letters so she could destroy them. Babbage, faithful to his deceased friend, refused to do so.

William carried out Ada's last wishes to the best of his capacity. In a final act of defiance against her mother's control, Ada had requested that her coffin should be buried in the Byron family vault, and that it should be placed so that it actually touched her father's own coffin. William ensured that this was done.

William married again, a decade after Ada's death. His second wife tried to heal the rift that had widened between him and his children since Ada's death, but she was not entirely successful. Ada's oldest child was so disgusted by the aristocracy that he changed his name, did his best to ignore his title as a lord, and spent his life working hard as a laborer. He died of tuberculosis at the age of twenty-six, still estranged from his father, and detested by Lady Byron, in whose opinion he had a revolting love for "low" company. Ada's youngest child, Ralph, inherited the title after his brother's death, and became a member of the House of Lords. Ralph, who had been raised in his grandmother's home, refused to speak to his father (because Lady Byron had successfully poisoned Ralph's mind against William) and the two remained estranged. Ada's daughter, Annabella, inherited her mother's brilliant mind, married an aristocratic gentleman, and lived a happy life.

Ada's lasting legacy to the world, however, was the academic work she had referred to as her "first child." Early scholars downplayed the importance and level of her notes, but in 1954, a researcher rediscovered them and understood the significance of her contribution, which included the first-ever computer program and a far-reaching original analysis of the capabilities of the computer (a machine that was never built in her time).

In 1890, a punch-card computing machine was used in the United States for sorting and tabulating information for the United States Census, echoing the usefulness of punch cards envisioned by Ada and Babbage in the operation of their machine. In 1931, decades after Babbage had come up with a concept of an Analytical Engine, the first "modern large analog" computer was built at the Massachusetts Institute of Technology. Shortly thereafter, in 1946, the first digital computer, ENIAC, was built.

In 1974, the United States Department of Defense decided to use one computer language for all its tasks. By then, many computer scientists considered Ada to be the first-ever computer programmer. In recognition, the military language was named Ada. On the 165th anniversary of Ada's birth, they created the Ada Joint Program Office, and the language was approved by the American National Institute as a nationwide all-purpose standard. It was given the document number MIL-STD-1815, in honor of the year of Ada's birth.

ENIAC, the first digital computer
(Courtesy of U.S. Army)

timeline

1815   Born December 10 in London, England.

1816   Mother, Lady Byron separates from husband, the
poet Lord Byron; Byron leaves Britain.

1833   Meets Charles Babbage.

1835   Marries William, Lord King.

1843   Begins translation of Menabrea's article on
Analytical Engine, adds substantial and original
"Notes" to the article.

1843   Translation and notes are published in *Taylor's
Scientific Memoirs*.

1850   Visits Lord Byron's ancestral home, Newstead Abbey.

1851   Diagnosed with cancer.

1852   Requests Babbage to be the executor of will; dies at
age thirty-six, buried beside father.

1980   United States Department of Defense names
common military high-order computer language
"Ada" in honor of Augusta Ada Byron, Countess
of Lovelace.

five
Sonya Kovalevsky

Sonya Korvin-Krukovsky Kovalevsky was born in Moscow on January 15, 1850, according to her closest friend and biographer, Anna Carlotta Leffler, duchess of Cajanello. Sonya was the middle child in her family, between older sister Aniuta and younger brother Fedya. Sonya claimed that her parents neglected her and focused their attention and affection on her siblings, leaving her with a feeling of deep insecurity.

Her father was a Russian army general: a proud patriarch and disciplinarian, he did not flinch from having his servants, male or female, flogged. He terrified the entire family when he was in a rage. Sonya wrote that while he was remarkably tender and soft and petted and jested with his children when they were ill, "on ordinary occasions, when all were well, he stuck to the rule that 'a man must be severe,' and therefore was very sparing of his caresses."

When Sonya was about five years old, the family lived in a stately home in Kaluga, a city in Western Russia. Sonya spent most of her time in "a spacious, but low-ceilinged room"—a nursery which she shared with her two siblings. The children were brought up largely by the nurse and a French governess. In Sonya's own words, the picture that presented itself every time she tried to recall the earliest years of her life was this: "A chiming of bells. An odor of incense. A throng of people comes out of the church. Nurse leads me by the hand from the church porch, carefully shielding me from being jostled."

Sonya was her nurse's favorite, but the kindly nurse had her prejudices (undoubtedly shared and encouraged by Sonya's parents): she refused to let Sonya play with children whom she considered to be beneath Sonya's social status. At that time, Russian society was stratified, and the servant class or serfs were often treated badly by the upper-class gentry (to which Sonya's father belonged).

Sonya's mother only looked in on her children occasionally. Sonya recalled that her mother was a "very handsome woman . . . always very merry, and handsomely dressed." Somehow, Sonya's awkward attempts to cuddle with her mother resulted in her hurting her mother "or tearing her gown" which made the little girl then "run away and hide myself in the corner with shame." Her nervousness was heightened by stories she overheard her nurse and other adults repeat: that she had been an unwanted girl, that her parents disliked her, and that when she was born, "the master and mistress were so chagrined, that they wouldn't look at her." Sonya possessed remarkable mental abilities as well as physical attractiveness, but she remained reserved and awkward in the presence of others.

When Sonya was about six years old, her father retired and the family settled on their vast country estate at Palibino—a remote corner of Russia near the Lithuanian border. There, Sonya's father "suddenly made the unexpected discovery that his children were not such models, such beautifully educated children, as he had supposed" and "decided upon a radical reform in the system of our education . . . two new persons were taken into the house—a Polish tutor and an English governess."

"The tutor was a quiet, learned man, who gave splendid lessons," but the strict governess had a greater impact on Sonya. Sonya was "the center and goal of all her thoughts and cares, and gave a meaning to her life; but her love . . . was oppressive, jealous, exacting, and utterly devoid of tenderness." This, combined with the conviction that ran "through all the memories of my childhood, like a black thread . . . that I was not beloved in the family" also made her develop an early craving "for a strong and exclusive affection" which she never outgrew.

Although her "governess did not approve of this occupation," little Sonya was so fascinated with "the very rhythm of verse" that from the age of five, she grew "passionately fond of poetry," and began writing her own. By the time she was twelve, Sonya was convinced that she "was destined to become a poet." Indeed, Sonya became an accomplished writer in addition to becoming a mathematician. In a letter written in 1890, Sonya commented on a similarity between the world of letters and the world of numbers; it seemed to her that the poet must see what others do not see, must see more deeply than other people, and that the mathematician must do the same.

As Sonya's interest in literature was not encouraged by her parents or her governess, she found herself "in a chronic state of book-hunger." However, she was influenced greatly by her sister Aniuta's attitudes and behavior. Sonya wrote that she "admired her beyond measure . . . and . . . would have gone through fire and water" for Aniuta. When Sonya was about ten and Aniuta was about sixteen, Aniuta began to yearn for more intellectual pursuits than she had access to on the country estate. Aniuta boldly went to their father, and requested that she be allowed to go to Petersburg to study. Their father "shouted at her as if she had been a small child. 'If you don't understand that it is the duty of every respectable girl to live with her parents until she marries, I won't argue with a stupid, bad little girl!'"

The governess, too, took sides against Anuita and "became watchful, and distrustfully spied upon every step she took." Sonya "felt instinctively that Aniuta had acquired some new and hitherto unprecedented interests, and . . . had a passionate desire to understand precisely what it was all about." Sonya began to quarrel with the governess on her sister's behalf, and the governess, "after one particularly stormy scene . . . announced that she would no longer stay." After the governess departed, Aniuta and Sonya drew closer.

Aniuta confided to Sonya that she had, in secret, started to write fiction. She had submitted a story to *The Epoch Magazine* and Fyodor Dostoevsky, the famous Russian novelist who edited the magazine, had accepted her work for publication. When Aniuta's father discovered that his daughter was writing, he was at first enraged, but he later consented to allow the family to take a winter trip to Petersburg to meet Dostoevsky.

When she was thirteen, Sonya met Russian novelist Fyodor
Dostoevsky, who praised her poetry.

Sonya wrote ecstatically of the journey:

> From the top of the carriage hangs a small traveling-lantern . . .
> Fantastic silver patterns start out on the windows of the carriage;
> the sleigh-bells jingle incessantly . . . All at once consciousness
> dawns on the mind with a bright gleam . . . and so much that is
> good and new which awaits us . . . soul is filled to overflowing
> with engrossing, dazzling happiness!

Aniuta proudly showed Sonya's work to Dostoevsky when they met, and Dostoevsky read Sonya's early poems and praised them. Thirteen-year-old Sonya developed a crush on Dostoevsky during their stay in Petersburg. Sonya quickly recovered from her crush, but the trip left a deep impression on her and her sister. Sonya ended her "Recollections of Childhood" by describing the end of this trip and the impact it had: "A feeling of reckless, unbounded joy in life overpowered us both. Heavens! How that life which lay before us attracted us, and beckoned us on; and how illimitable, how mysterious, and how beautiful it seemed to us that night!"

The seeds of independence planted in Sonya and her sister strengthened into a fierce determination to pursue their intellectual passions. In Sonya's case, though her love of poetry and literature remained all her life, it was matched if not surpassed by her intoxication with mathematics.

Early in her life, Sonya formed "particularly strong attachments" for two of her uncles who encouraged in her an interest in science and mathematics. Her maternal uncle, Feodor Fedorovitch Schubert, was impressed with her cleverness and spent a lot of time with her on his visits, giving her "scientific lectures."

Her eldest paternal uncle, Pyotr Vasilevitch Korvin-Krukovsky shared her love of books. The "library was his favorite nook," his "one sole weakness was reading to excess, to the verge of insanity," and he "was carried away most of all when he came upon the description of some new scientific discovery." Sonya and her uncle sat "together for hours at a time . . . forgetful that he was addressing a child, he frequently developed . . . the most abstract theories" before her, and she was so pleased that she did her best to understand him.

"Although he had never studied mathematics, he cherished the most profound respect for that science. He had gathered a certain amount of mathematical knowledge from various books" and he often discussed mathematical concepts with Sonya, imbuing her with "a reverence for mathematics, as for a very lofty and mysterious science, which opened out to those who consecrated themselves to it a new and wonderful world not to be attained by simple mortals." These were some of Sonya's "first encounters with the domain of mathematics."

Another incident also awakened Sonya's mathematical interest. One of the rooms in the house set aside for the use of the children was not properly wallpapered. Instead, "by a happy accident" the paper consisted of sheets which seemed to Sonya to be "speckled over with some kind of hieroglyphics" that attracted her attention. She "would stand by the wall for hours on end, reading and rereading what was written there," and she eventually came to understand the walls were covered with lithographed lectures on differential and integral calculus. "As a result of my sustained scrutiny I learned many of the writings by heart," she said, and the formulae were almost engraved on Sonya's memory, although at the moment of reading she could not understand them. "The depth of that impression was evidenced several years later," when, as a fifteen-year-old, she "was taking lessons from Professor A. N. Strannolyubsky in Petersburg . . . he was astounded at the speed with which" she assimilated the study of calculus.

Sonya attributed to tutor Yosif Ignatievich Malevich her "first systematic study of mathematics." Although his lessons were only a "dim recollection" to her in later years, she wrote "there is no question that they influenced me very much and were important in my later development." Malevitch taught

Sonya arithmetic, elementary geometry, and algebra. Sonya was not fascinated with arithmetic, because under her uncle Pyotr's influence, she was "much more taken with various abstract considerations—infinity, for example." All through her life, it was "the philosophical aspect of mathematics" that attracted Sonya the most, and it was only as Sonya grew familiar with algebra that she began to feel "an attraction to mathematics so intense" that she neglected her other studies.

Noticing Sonya's fascination with mathematics, her father, "who in any case harbored a strong prejudice against learned women—decided that it was high time to put a stop to" her mathematical lessons with Malevich. But somehow Sonya managed "to wheedle out of my teacher a copy of Bourdon's *Algebra Course* and began studying it with diligence."

Sonya said later that her mathematical knowledge may have remained confined for a long time to the contents of this one textbook, however, had she not been aided by a visit from a family friend, Professor Tyrtov, which motivated her father to reassess his views on Sonya's mathematical education. Professor Tytrov gifted the family a copy of an elementary physics text book that he had written. Sonya attempted to read it, but to her "chagrin . . . encountered trigonometric formulas, sines, cosines and tangents. What was a sine?" She turned to her tutor for help, but "he replied that he did not know what a sine was. Then, trying to cope with the formulas contained in the book, I tried to explain it for myself." Grappling with the problem, she answered it using "the same road that had been taken historically: that is, instead of a sine . . . used a chord." She told Professor Tyrtov how much his book had interested her, and explained the approach she had taken to understanding trigonometric functions. The Professor was impressed by Sonya's mathematical ability:

> He went straight to my father heatedly arguing the necessity of providing me with the most serious kind of instruction, and even comparing me to Pascal. After some hesitation, my father agreed to have me taught by Professor Strannolyubsky, with whom I then settled down to work successfully. In the course of that winter I went through analytic geometry, differential and integral calculus.

During Sonya's childhood, Russia had experienced a brief liberalizing movement. In 1860, Russian universities received a certain degree of autonomy, and women students were permitted to attend some lectures. Unfortunately, in 1862, the Petersburg University was closed because of student unrest, and by the time it reopened, women were barred from admittance to universities. So by the time Sonya was in her late teens, there was nearly no hope of higher education or a professional career for Sonya in Russia. It was not easy to go abroad to places that were less hostile to women pursuing higher studies, either. Russian women were not issued passports in their own names, but had to have permission from their fathers or husbands to travel abroad. Sonya's father, like most Russian parents, would never consider allowing their daughters to study abroad.

Many young Russian women who wanted to pursue their intellectual interests resorted to a creative solution: they found liberal men who would consent to a marriage of convenience. These husbands would then give their wives the freedom they wished to have, and the couple would go their separate ways. Sonya and her sister were determined to study, and they decided that one of them would marry, and the other would either marry or accompany the new couple out of Russia and into Europe. They found a young publisher called Vladimir Kovalevsky, who was willing to help them out by marrying Sonya. Sonya's father, who may have suspected that this was a sham, resisted the arrangement. Sonya came up with a clever ploy to force him to cooperate: when he was in the company of distinguished guests, she let it be known that she and her fiancé were busy preparing for their wedding. Rather than publicly admit that his daughter was acting against his wishes, General Krukovsky reluctantly announced the engagement. Sonya's rebellion went further: she ran away to Vladimir's apartment and refused to leave until her parents agreed to the marriage.

Sonya was married in September 1868, at the age of seventeen. The couple moved to Petersburg and Sonya attended lectures on a variety of subjects, before concentrating on mathematics. Early the next year, they left Russia and traveled to Vienna, and then to Heidelberg.

Heidelberg University was not as easy to enter as Sonya had dreamed. She had to go from one professor to another, until finally, a special commission came together to decide whether she could attend lectures. It decided against allowing her to attend every lecture, but agreed that she could apply to individual professors, who could decide to let her into their lectures at their discretion.

In the fall of 1870, Sonya left Heidelberg for the University of Berlin, where she had much greater success. She hoped that good recommendations from her teachers in Heidelberg would help persuade the famous mathematician Karl Weierstrass to take her on as a student despite her otherwise sparse mathematical background. Later, Sonya wrote that she considered

A view of Heidelberg, where Sonya attempted to attend lectures at the university, but was met with opposition.

Weierstrass "one of the greatest mathematicians of all time . . . He gave a completely new direction to the entire discipline of mathematics and created—not in Germany alone but in other countries as well—a whole school of young scholars who follow the road he marked out to develop his ideas." She was adamant to have him as her mentor, and showing the determination that had helped her succeed in her desire to study abroad, she petitioned him to take her on as his student.

Before deciding whether to help Sonya, Weierstrass tested her abilities by giving her a list of mathematical problems to solve. Sonya's solutions impressed him so deeply that

Famous mathematician Karl Weierstrass became Sonya's mentor at the University of Berlin.

he agreed to give her weekly lessons in private (because at that time the University of Berlin forbade women from attending lectures).

Between 1870 and 1871, Sonya immersed herself in mathematics. Vladimir was elsewhere, working on his dissertation. In the spring of 1871, Aniuta, who was still very close to Sonya, was living with her common-law husband in Paris. After a brief episode, when Sonya and Vladimir went to support the couple who became involved with a political struggle in Paris at the time, Sonya returned to Berlin and resumed her studies with Weierstrass.

In a letter that Weierstrass wrote to Sonya in January of 1872, he requested her to send back a paper that he needed to use in his next lecture, clearly showing that by then, Sonya had made up for her incomplete early mathematical training and already caught up with the male university students that Weierstrass taught regularly. Weierstrass and Sonya became very close. By November 1872, Weierstrass was addressing Sonya as "Du" in his letters, which is the informal term for "you" in German, rather than the formal form "*sie*," and referring to her as a "*freundin*" or dear friend, not a "*schulerin*" or pupil. His letters to her also indicated that Sonya had confided in him, both that her marriage was only one of convenience, and that she wished to obtain her doctorate in mathematics.

The doors of the University of Berlin were closed to Sonya as a woman, so she determined to try for her doctorate at the University of Goettingen, which had a more liberal attitude toward women. Between November 1872 and August 1874, Sonya stayed in Berlin and worked on her doctoral dissertation. But instead of completing the one dissertation required by regulations, she "completed three: two in pure mathematics . . . and the third on a topic in astronomy . . . All three works were presented to the University of Goettingen."

A building on the campus of the University of Goettingen, which awarded Sonya a doctoral degree based on her mathematical achievements. (*Courtesy of imagebroker/Alamy*)

Weierstrass asked for her to be awarded the degree without the customary oral examination and her work was so innovative that the faculty agreed to do so, overlooking the fact that she had never attended classes at the University of Goettingen. Sonya was not only awarded her doctoral degree, but also, based on the strength and depth and breadth of her achievements that far surpassed ordinary requirements, the doctorate was awarded summa cum laude (with highest honors). In requesting a doctoral degree for Sonya, Weierstrass made it clear that his involvement was minimal, and ensured that she was accorded full credit for the individuality and creativity of her work. In 1874, when the independence of Sonya's work was questioned, Weierstrass clarified in a letter to the mathematician Du Bois-Reymond, "Except for correcting her numerous grammatical mistakes, I did not do anything other than formulate the problem . . . I did not expect any result different to what is known from the theory of ordinary differential equations . . . This is not true, as you can see . . . in the dissertation. This was discovered, to my great surprise, by my student completely independently . . . the seemingly simple means she found to overcome the obstacle I value highly as proof of her mathematical flair."

Sonya's doctoral dissertation on calculus, "*Zur Theorie der partiellen Differentialgleichungen*" (Towards a Theory of Partial Differential Equations) was published in *Crelle's Journal*. "This honor, given to very few mathematicians is particularly great for a novice in the field, inasmuch as *Crelle's Journal* was then regarded as the most serious mathematics publication in Germany. The best scientific minds of the day contributed to it," she later remembered.

The dissertation contained the proof for a theorem that had been produced in 1842 by the mathematician Cauchy. Neither Sonya nor Weierstrass knew of Cauchy's work. The proof Sonya independently arrived at for the theorem was simpler than Cauchy's. Poincare, a mathematician whom Sonya later described as one of the two "most gifted of the new generation of mathematicians in all of Europe," said that Sonya's work had given the theorem its definitive form. Her work was widely considered more comprehensive, profound, and sophisticated than Cauchy's. This theorem, named the Cauchy-Kovalevsky theorem, is now a part of all basic courses in mathematical analysis.

The other pure mathematics dissertation that Sonya submitted, *"Ueber die Reduction einer bestimmten Klasse Abel'scher Integrale 3-en Ranges auf elliptische Integrale"* (On the reduction of a class of Abelian integrals of the third rank to elliptical integrals) was published in 1884 in *Acta Mathematica*. Tackling this problem required a deep understanding of the theory of Abelian functions, which is considered one of the most difficult theories in mathematical analysis. Her third doctoral dissertation, which dealt with the mathematics behind the form of the planet Saturn's rings, was published in 1885 in the journal *Astronomische Nachrichten*. This work was entitled *"Zusaetze und Bermerkungen zu Laplace's Untersuchungen ueber die Gestalt der Saturnsringe"* (Supplements and remarks on Laplace's investigation of the form of Saturn's ring). Sonya, by operating under a different assumption from French mathematician Pierre-Simon de Laplace's, obtained a correction to his solution. Modern concepts of Saturn's rings are quite different from that imagined by Laplace and Sonya, but nevertheless, Sonya's insights into the mathematics of the equations she investigated and the calculations she conducted are of great theoretical value.

Sonya's work on all three problems was thorough and remarkable, and in Weierstrass's opinion, any one of her three dissertations alone would have been more than sufficient for obtaining her doctoral degree.

Around 1873, Sonya, who had lived together with Vladimir off and on ever since the beginning of their marriage, fell unexpectedly in love with her husband. This was probably in part because Vladimir who was more attracted to Sonya than she had initially realized, had persistently tried to win her over. In a letter written to her sister in September 1868, she had confided "you won't believe how he cares about me, courts me, and is ready to submit his every desire and habit to mine . . . I love him truly with all my heart, but as I would my younger brother." Sonya's love evolved, however, and after her dissertation was completed, the couple planned their future together. Sometime during the next few years, they finally consummated their marriage.

In 1874, Sonya and Vladimir returned to Russia. There, she worked "far less zealously than . . . in Germany and . . . the situation was far less propitious for scholarly work . . . work was punctuated by long and frequent interruptions" and Sonya barely managed to keep abreast of developments in her field. She did not complete a single independent study during this period of residence in Russia, and wrote that the only thing that still gave her "some feeling of scholarly support was the exchange of letters and ideas" with her beloved teacher, Weierstrass.

Sonya felt distracted from serious work by Russian society and the conditions under which she had to live. She and Vladimir were disillusioned by the lack of respect accorded to them despite their doctoral degrees. Both had difficulty finding jobs that attracted them. "At that time all of Russian society was pervaded by the spirit of profit-making and by the emergence of various commercial enterprises," and the frustrated couple finally began to speculate in real estate, hoping that they would become wealthy enough to then pursue their scholarly interests. Unfortunately, the commercial ventures they tried resulted in failure.

Among other things, Sonya's interest in writing resurfaced, and she began writing theater reviews for the Russian newspaper *Novoye vremya* (*New Times*). She also enjoyed immersing herself in society, and the couple led an active social life. They met many eminent mathematicians and writers. Sonya later wrote a novel, entitled *Nigilistika* (*Nihilist girl* or *The Nihilist*), which was published in 1892, and begins in an almost autobiographical manner, with her heroine saying:

> I was twenty-two years old when I moved to Petersburg. Three months earlier I had graduated from a university abroad and returned to Russia, doctoral degree in hand . . . life in Petersburg immediately enveloped, and, as it were, intoxicated me. Putting aside for a while the consideration of analytic functions, space, and the four dimensions, which had so recently obsessed me, I threw myself into new interests. I made acquaintances left and right. I tried to penetrate the most varied circles . . . It was a time when everything interested and pleased me . . . Theaters, benefit galas, and literary circles with their endless discussions of every kind of abstract topic ultimately leading nowhere . . . I surrendered to them with all the passion of a naturally talkative

Russian who had spent five years among German ways in the sole company of two or three specialists.

Although Sonya wrote to Weierstrass that she had been straying from mathematics, he remained certain that she would return to the field. He wrote encouragingly, "I am even not very much disconcerted when you write that this is how matters stand: partly because I am convinced that a certain distraction will not harm you after such long work, partly because I am firmly sure that your serious mind and your attraction to ideal aspirations will not allow you to restrain from research too long." Weierstrass's unshakeable faith in Sonya proved accurate.

In October 1878, Sonya gave birth to a daughter, named Sophia Vladimirovna Kovalevskaya, nicknamed Fufa. During this period, Sonya also wrote a novel which was translated into several languages.

Despite their happiness at their daughter's birth, 1879 was a difficult year for the couple. Vladimir was deeply affected by their financial disasters, the lack of an academic position, and worst of all, by the fact that some of his acquaintances suspected him of being a spy. He began to withdraw from their social circle.

In contrast, Sonya threw herself once again into mathematics, despite the demands on her as a young mother. She met the Russian mathematician Chebyshev, and, with his encouragement, presented a paper at the Sixth Congress of Mathematicians and Physicians, which was held between late December 1879 and early January 1880. At the conference, she met Goesta Mittag-Leffler, who had, earlier, been a student of Weierstrass. Mittag-Leffler was so impressed by Sonya

Goesta Mittag-Leffler, Sonya's good friend, managed to secure a university teaching position for Sonya in Sweden.

that upon his return to Sweden, where he was a professor, he began to petition the university to award Sonya an academic position.

In 1880, Vladimir and Sonya moved to Moscow, hoping to secure academic positions at the university there. However, Vladimir was still distracted by business ventures, and their marital relationship grew increasingly strained. At the end of the year, Sonya went to Berlin, where she met Weierstrass again to recharge herself with her passion for mathematics, before returning to Moscow in January 1881. That spring, she moved to Berlin with her daughter, but Vladimir went to visit his brother in another part of Russia.

Mittag-Leffler's efforts to secure an academic position for Sonya met with failure, more because of her nationality than her gender, in his opinion. However, Weierstrass gave Sonya a new mathematical project to work on, regarding the refraction of light in crystals. Soon after beginning this project, Sonya also gained new insights into another problem that had interested her earlier: the equations which describe the motion of a rotating rigid body, to which a satisfactory general solution had not yet been found.

Alone in Russia, Vladimir was depressed by his financial misfortunes and wrote requesting Sonya to return to living with him, suggesting tactlessly that she was wasting her time on mathematics because no woman had yet achieved anything in the field. She replied that it was precisely because of that she felt she had to put herself in a position where she could demonstrate whether she could achieve anything or whether she did not have brains enough for that. Despite her marital difficulties, Sonya wrote affectionately to Vladimir throughout the summer of 1881, even assuring him that she was willing to return to Russia and resume their life together as a family, after she finished her work.

Sonya underestimated the time it would take for her to complete her work on the two problems she was trying to solve. Vladimir grew impatient as he waited for her to return. In early 1882, he came to Paris to meet her but agreed to return to Russia alone and try to straighten out their finances. Upon his return, Vladimir found that he was too far in debt to resolve the situation, and that his partners had defrauded him and even tricked him into a position where he would almost certainly be held legally responsible for fraud that they had committed. He tried to keep this situation a secret from Sonya, but Sonya misinterpreted this behavior, thinking he wanted to distance himself from her. She grew somewhat cooler toward him. In April 1883, Vladimir committed suicide.

When Sonya learned of his death, she blamed herself. She was so shocked and depressed that she locked herself away and refused to eat or drink, lapsing into a coma after five days. Fortunately, her friends supported and nursed her back to health with a doctor's assistance. Finally, Sonya recovered mentally and physically, and prepared herself to untangle the financial situation left behind by Vladimir and to clear his name of the legal charges against him.

Sonya returned to Russia, to stay with her brother-in-law, but she also somehow found the strength and determination to travel to Berlin and successfully finish her mathematical research. She later recalled "my work was completed in 1883 and had something of an impact in the mathematical world, for the problem of light refraction had not yet been satisfactorily clarified and I had viewed it from a different, entirely new standpoint. This paper of mine was published in 1884." Sonya also managed to establish Vladimir's innocence and straighten out his affairs; however, for the rest of her life, she felt morally obliged to repay various people who claimed that the couple owed them money. Obtaining a position as a university professor was her only remaining hope for some level of financial security.

Urged by Weierstrass, Mittag-Leffler resumed his efforts to secure an academic position for Sonya in Sweden. In 1883, he invited Sonya to come to Stockholm and teach at the university, and in November of that year, Sonya sailed abroad again, leaving her daughter in the care of a friend. Mittag-Leffler advised her to bring Fufa along so that she would be respected by the conventional women of Stockholm society, but Sonya refused quite flatly, saying that in serious matters, when not only her well-being but that of her child was involved, she would consider it an unforgivable weakness on her part if she allowed herself to be influenced even slightly by the wish to *appear* a good mother.

The Lefflers were extremely kind and welcoming. Later, Sonya told Mittag-Leffler that she thought his friendship was the best she had had in all her life. Mittag-Leffler's wife,

Anna, also became one of Sonya's closest friends, and wrote Sonya's biography after Sonya's death.

Mittag-Leffler was taking a risk by asking Sonya to lecture, as she was not established as a full-fledged faculty member and had no teaching experience at all. On January 30, 1884, Sonya gave her first lecture in German on partial differential equations. By this time, she had mastered German and French, in addition to Russian, but it was, nevertheless, her third language, at best. Mittag-Leffler observed joyously in a letter to Weierstrass that the auditorium was full, because people were well aware of the historic nature of the occasion—the first female Ph.D. in mathematics was making her first appearance in a university lecture hall.

She was nervous and stumbled at first, but finished her talk to applause. From this first session, it was clear to Mittag-Leffler and the others that she would be a good lecturer. After Sonya successfully delivered her first special course in mathematics, less than a year after her first lecture, she was appointed professor at Stockholm University for five years. Within a year, Sonya was able to deliver her lectures in Swedish.

Despite her academic success, however, Sonya still suffered from feelings of isolation. In her diary, she recorded, "Gave the first lecture today. Don't know whether it was good or bad, but I know that it was very sad to go home and feel so lonely in this world. I feel especially lonely at such times. *Encore une etape de la vie derriere moi.* (Yet another stage of life is behind me)." Her depression did not, however, keep her from doing diligent research, in addition to teaching and mentoring students, especially other young women.

During the first year of her residence in Sweden, she began to work, among other things, on what she later referred to as the most important of her mathematical contributions. She examined the problem of the rotation of a solid body around a fixed point, under the influence of gravity. She wrote:

> The problem, which encompasses the theory of the pendulum, is a highly significant one. It is also one of the classical problems of mathematics; some of the greatest minds, including Euler, Lagrange and Poisson have applied their efforts to its solution . . . In the whole history of mathematics there are not many problems like this one—in such compelling need of solution, to which so much intellectual power and stubborn labor have been applied without leading to substantive results in the majority of cases . . . the Paris Academy of Science announced a prize competition for the best essay '*Sur le probleme de la rotation d'un corps solide autour d'un point fixe*' with the proviso that the essay must substantially refine or supplement findings previously attained in this area of mechanics.

When the competition was announced, Sonya had already achieved the main results of her research on the subject. She worked zealously to put her material in order, work out the details, and submit a manuscript to the competition before the June 1, 1888, deadline.

In the summer of 1886, Aniuta, whose health had been failing for some time, took a turn for the worse. Sonya traveled to Russia to see her. After spending time with her sister, Sonya returned to Sweden along with her daughter. The 1886-1887 academic year was filled with difficult challenges. Sonya had to take care of Fufa, and keep up with her research and teaching, while worrying about her sister. That autumn, Aniuta's health worsened further and Sonya asked for a leave of absence to return to Russia to nurse her sister back to health. Her request was refused by the university, and most male professors considered it an impertinence. They did not try to understand the conflict Sonya faced between career and family.

As the pioneering female professor of mathematics at a European university, Sonya was among the first to face a problem that afflicts many career women. She was constantly forced to prove her devotion to her profession. Although she enjoyed the support of many male colleagues, the academic environment as a whole was hostile to women.

In the spring of 1887, Sonya came up with the idea for a play, and began to write it together with Mittag-Leffler's sister. Mittag-Leffler was exasperated to see Sonya pursuing literary interests that distracted her from mathematics. In his opinion, they were a waste of time. He need not have worried. Although Sonya spent some time writing plays and novels during her time in Sweden, she remained most active in mathematical research.

In the fall of 1887, Aniuta died. Sonya, who had always cherished a close bond with her sister, was grief stricken. In her loneliness, she turned to men for comfort; one of them was an old acquaintance called Maxim. Afraid that this relationship would prevent Sonya from submitting her work in a timely manner to the Paris Academy's competition, Mittag-Leffler persuaded Maxim to leave Stockholm for a while. After Maxim left, Sonya concentrated hard on her work, aiming for the summer 1888 deadline. She discussed the theory for an asymmetrical body, where the center of its mass is not on an axis in the body. This piece of work, sometimes called the "Kovalevskaya top" is still of interest to mathematical physicists.

By the rules of the competition, called the *Prix Bordin*, all entries had to be submitted anonymously. The outcome was unprecedented. Sonya's paper "was found deserving of the prize. And that was not all: in view of the fact that the same topic had been assigned three times running and had remained unsolved each time, and also in view of the significance of the results achieved, the Academy voted to increase the previously announced award of 3000 francs to 5000. The envelope was then unsealed." The judging committee was astonished to discover that the prize winner was a woman. Sonya had solved as much of the problem as anyone could reasonably hope to do, far surpassing previous work as well as the committee's expectations of what was possible. Sonya was informed, and she immediately left for Paris, where she "was given a highly ceremonial reception and seated next to the president, who made a flattering speech; all in all, honors were lavished upon" her.

Maxim accompanied her to the celebratory events and Sonya was infatuated with him, but their relationship was strained. Despite her triumphs, Sonya confided to Mittag-Leffler in 1889 that she had never felt so depressed before in her life. She described herself as unhappy as a dog, and then added that for dogs' sakes she hoped they could not be as unhappy as she could be. Soon after, she applied for a leave of absence for reasons of health and asked Mittag-Leffler to support her request. Although Mittag-Leffler was trying to get her five-year contract at that time, he helped her secure this leave of absence.

In May 1889, the University of Stockholm made Sonya a full professor for life. That same year, she also received a prize from the Swedish Academy of Sciences for her remarkable mathematical contributions and saw the publication of a Swedish edition of her novel, *The Sisters Raevsky (or Memories of Childhood)*. But Sonya was suffering from nervous exhaustion and needed time away. For the first nine months of the year she used her leave of absence to travel, meeting Maxim whenever she could. Maxim was not a very supportive partner; he had refused to relocate to Sweden to be with her, and had difficulty accepting her celebrity status. In fall 1889, Sonya returned to the university.

Some of Sonya's Russian colleagues wished that she would return to the country of her birth. She was made a corresponding member of the Russian Academy of Sciences in 1889, and she traveled to Petersburg, while retaining her professorship in Sweden. She found that many Russians were still prejudiced against women, and some jealous male colleagues even stated publicly (and unjustifiably) that her work was filled with errors. When Sonya challenged them to show where she had erred, they could not do so. Her name was proposed for nomination as a full member of the Academy, but the prevailing chauvinistic attitude prevented her from being elected to this richly deserved honor.

In September 1890, Sonya wrote that she was happily immersed in mathematical research, and told her friend and colleague Henri Poincaré that she was sending a letter to their mutual mathematician friend Charles Hermite, describing new results that she had discovered on the rotation problem. Unfortunately many of the letters Hermite received were destroyed in a fire, and the letter to which Sonya referred was never found.

After the fall term in 1890, Sonya traveled to Genoa. She spent the winter holidays with Maxim. On her return from this trip, she fell ill. Nevertheless, she managed to teach her first class of the new term on Friday, February 6, before taking to her bed. The following Monday, she described her plans for further work on the Euler equations, but early the next morning, on Tuesday February 10, 1891, Sonya died of pneumonia. She was just forty-one years old.

The news of Sonya's sudden death shocked the many intellectuals she had interacted with during her short life: among them many renowned mathematicians, artists, and writers of the time. Sonya's contributions were significant in themselves, but she also had a large impact in mathematics because she acted as a link between the mathematical work that was being conducted in Western Europe and the work being done in Russia. Sonya had become the first female Ph. D. in mathematics, the first woman on the editorial staff of a mathematical journal, and the first woman to hold a chair at her university. She had published numerous original papers before her untimely death.

Even after Sonya's death, her work continued to appear in print. Her novella, *Nigilistika*, was published posthumously in 1892 in Geneva with an introduction by Maxim. It was reprinted by several publishers, though it was banned in Tsarist Russia and only published in the Soviet Union in 1928. Another version of the book was published in 1893 in a collection titled *Vera Vorontsova*. Sonya also left behind two unfinished novels, in addition to her several published literary pieces in magazines and newspapers.

Kronecker, a German mathematician said that the history of mathematics would speak of her as one of the rarest investigators. However, perhaps because of her gender, Sonya Kovalevsky is not nearly as well known as she ought to be, despite her astounding record of staggering achievements.

timeline

1850   Born in Moscow, January 15.

1868   Married to Vladimir Kovalevsky.

1874   Becomes first European woman to receive a doctorate in mathematics (granted by the University of Goettingen).

1878   Gives birth to daughter.

1883   Husband commits suicide in spring; presents a paper on the refraction of light in a crystalline medium at the scientific congress in Odessa in September; leaves for Stockholm in November to lecture on the theory of partial differential equations.

1884   Officially appointed professor of Mathematics at the University of Stockholm.

1888   Receives the *Prix Bordin* of the French Academy of Sciences in recognition of work *On the Problem of Rotation of a Solid Body about a Fixed Point.*

1891   Dies in Stockholm, Sweden.

six

Emmy Noether

I n 1964, at a World Fair, one room was devoted to survey of the history of mathematics. Of the eighty pictures of mathematicians displayed on the walls, only one was of a woman. That woman was Emmy Noether. One of the most influential mathematicians of the twentieth century, Amalie Emmy Noether's contributions to mathematics and theoretical physics are immense. Yet, although her work is considered by some to be among the greatest of the twentieth century, as fundamental in importance to our understanding of how the universe works as Einstein's, and as essential to twentieth century science as his famous ideas, her name is not nearly as well recognized as his.

Emmy, the daughter of Ida Amalia Kaufmann and Max Noether, was born in Erlangen, Germany, in 1882. Her parents were prosperous, highly intellectual Jews. Her father, Max Noether, was afflicted with polio during his childhood.

A 1916 view of Erlangen, Germany

However, he overcame this disability and went on to become a mathematics professor, first at the University of Heidelberg, and later at the University of Erlangen. Max Noether was one of the founders of nineteenth-century algebraic geometry. He helped lay the foundations of mathematics that later served as the language in which Einstein was able to express his theory of general relativity.

Emmy had a happy childhood. She was nearsighted and had a slight lisp when she spoke, and her warm, easygoing nature endeared her to her many friends, as well as to her teachers. She attended the *Stadtischen Hoheren Tochterschule* in Erlangen for eight years, beginning in 1889.

Her early life resembled that of most German girls of the times. She took piano lessons, but unlike her mother who was an accomplished musician, she preferred dancing to music (which she was not particularly good at). At first, she seemed set to enter a career as a language teacher. After secondary school, in the spring of 1900, Emmy successfully passed the Bavarian State Examinations for female teachers of French and English. At that point, she could have gone on to teach foreign languages at a women's school. But Emmy changed her mind. Although her early ambition had been to become a teacher, she announced that she wanted to continue her studies at a university.

Even at the University of Erlangen, where her father was a full professor, women were not permitted to study officially. However, sometimes exceptions were made and women were allowed to sit in on university courses unofficially, provided the instructor gave permission. In 1900, Emmy was granted special permission to attend lectures, and she began her course work. She was one of just two females, out of a total of 986 students. From 1900 to 1903 she sat in on lectures without receiving credit at the University of Erlangen.

In 1903, she passed the official *Reifepruefung* or *matura* examinations at the Koeniglisches Realgymnasium in Nuremberg (equivalent to completing a bachelor's degree in the United States). That winter, she registered as a student at the University of Goettingen, where she met many great mathematical minds of the day, including David Hilbert and Felix Klein. After her first semester at Goettingen, Emmy returned to the University of Erlangen, which had finally decided to legalize the enrollment and matriculation of women students. In October 1904, Emmy listed mathematics as her chosen field of study.

In December 1907, Emmy completed her doctoral dissertation, entitled *Ueber die Bildung des Formensystems der*

Felix Klein was one of the people Emmy made friends with at the University of Goettingen. *(Courtesy of Science Museum/SSPL /The Image Works)*

ternaeren biquadratischen Form (On Complete Systems of Invariants for Ternary Biquadratic Forms). Her *doctorvater* or mentor was Paul Gordon, a friend of her father's. The next year, her doctorate was awarded with the highest honors. The mathematical work she did for the university embodied one of her fundamental characteristics: she strove to find general formulations for mathematical questions. In this effort, she was helped by her amazing ability to strip a mathematical problem of any incidental complicating or obscuring detail, pare it down to its essence, and thus discover the precise formulation that revealed the logical nature of a question.

In 1908, she was also selected as a member of the Italian association, *Circolo Matematico di Palermo* (Mathematical Circle of Palermo), and became a member of the *Deutschen Mathematiker-Vereinigung* (German Association of Mathematicians). She devotedly attended the conferences held by these organizations, where she also presented her work.

After obtaining her doctorate, Emmy moved back from Goettingen to Erlangen to care for her aging father. She often substituted as a lecturer for him, as he found it increasingly difficult to move. Emmy wanted to become a professor, but the University of Erlangen had a policy against employing women as professors. She was allowed to teach, but was forced to do so unofficially, without being accorded a title or being paid for her work.

In 1914, Emmy completed a manuscript entitled *Koerper und Systeme rationaler Funktionen* [Fields and Systems of Rational Functions], which was later described by some as her most important paper from this period that she spent in Erlangen. Emmy stated that this work had been sparked by a discussion with the mathematician Ernst Fischer. Later, Emmy credited Fischer with having helped to start her on the path of abstract mathematical thinking.

Until 1915, Emmy worked at the Mathematical Institute in Erlangen without pay. She carried out independent mathematical research, attended conferences in her field, and presented her work and published mathematical papers. Yet, although the quality of her research was equal to or above that of most of her colleagues, her gender prevented her from finding a position worthy of her intelligence and expertise.

Luckily, at the University of Goettingen, Emmy had made friends with two influential mathematicians: Hilbert and Klein. In 1915, Hilbert and Klein, who respected Emmy's work, invited her to return to the University of Goettingen to teach and conduct research. They were not motivated purely by an unselfish desire to help her: they were also well aware that their own research would benefit from collaboration with Emmy. By having Emmy team up with them as a co-author on mathematical research papers, they could forge stronger and more creative ideas.

Goettingen was, at that time, considered the foremost German (if not European) mathematical research institute. Emmy accepted their invitation and returned to Goettingen. There, she received steadfast support and encouragement from these two colleagues, but most of the other faculty did not give her a warm welcome. Hilbert fought tirelessly, though in vain, to win Emmy a paid position, saying that he did not understand why her sex should be a valid argument against her admission to the faculty. After all, he said, the faculty senate was part of a university, not a bathing establishment. He met heavy opposition from the majority of the faculty. They argued that it would be disrespectful and unthinkable that German soldiers, returning from fighting in the world war that was raging (World War I), should find themselves being forced to learn at the feet of a woman. Emmy was neither worried nor deterred by the antagonistic attitude displayed by the university faculty. Taking a strong stand against popular opinion, Hilbert found a way for Emmy to lecture: he announced a course in his name, and then let her lecture instead. However, it was only a small victory, because she wasn't paid or officially recognized for her work. She was once again forced to accept an unsalaried position.

Undeterred by this injustice, Emmy threw herself into her work. During the earliest phase of Emmy's research career, her way of thinking was understandably influenced by what she had learned from her mentor Paul Gordon, a traditionalist. Gordon taught her a formal, algorithmic, constructive approach to mathematics. He had once exclaimed, upon reading a paper of Hilbert's, *"Das ist nicht Mathematik; das ist Theologie"* (This is not mathematics; this is Theology). Despite Gordon's criticism of Hilbert's views, Emmy came increasingly under Hilbert's influence in Goettingen, and she transitioned to using methods that were not based purely on computation. She later went so far as to disparage her dissertation (completed earlier under Gordon's mentorship), describing it by words such as: *"rechnerei"* (routine calculations) and *"formelngestruepp"* (jungle of formulae). Emmy's views were maturing into the most distinguishing characteristic of her work: her remarkable ability to synthesize and see extremely important generalities, and a sophisticated abstractness of approach.

Like many others in the math world, Emmy took an interest in the work of the young German mathematician, Albert Einstein. Shortly after arriving in Goettingen in 1915, she wrote to Fisher, *"Hilbert will naechste Woch ueber seine Einsteinschen Differentialinvarianten vortragen, und da muessen die Goettinger doch etwas koennen."* (Hilbert will lecture next week on his Einsteinian differential invariants, and to understand that, the people in Goettingen must certainly know something). By 1917, Emmy was interested in

Albert Einstein *(Library of Congress)*

the connections between Hilbert's invariant theory and Albert Einstein's relativity theory. She became involved with a project to develop the mathematical formulae to support Einstein's theory. By 1918, she had worked out a universal mathematical formulation for two of the most significant aspects of the general theory of relativity. Emmy's groundbreaking work was immediately recognized by Albert Einstein himself. In a letter to Hilbert, Einstein praised Emmy's penetrating mathematical insight and the vantage point she had provided: "Yesterday I received from Miss Noether a very interesting work about invariant forms. It impressed me, that one can comprehend these things from such a general standpoint. It wouldn't have hurt the old Guard at Goettingen, had they been schooled by Miss Noether. She certainly knows what she is doing."

That year, Emmy completed what was arguably her most profound and important piece of research: she proved a theorem which came to carry her name. Noether's theorem connects forces and motion and the fundamental laws of physics with the world of symmetry. It demonstrates how symmetry governs the physical process of the universe.

Visually, something is said to have symmetry when different parts of it look alike. For instance, faces have bilateral symmetry. If a line is drawn through the center of a person's face, on each side of the line there will be half a nose, one eye, half the mouth, and one ear in each half. This is a basic and simple idea of symmetry.

Mathematically, symmetry is an expression of equivalence or equality between things. When two things are essentially the same, the mathematical symbol = is used, indicating that the two things are equal (the same). In physics, the concept of symmetry may be expressed this way: if a physical system remains essentially the same after a change is made to it, the system is said to possess symmetry. Emmy Noether proved a mathematical theorem about nature, connecting a mathematical description of symmetry to symmetry found in physics.

Conservation laws are essential in physics. One example of a conservation law is the law of conservation of energy, which states that the total energy of a system doesn't change as a result of a physical process (i.e. that the total energy of the system before a physical process occurs is equal to the system's total energy after the physical process occurs). A similar law is the law of conservation of momentum, which states that the total momentum of a system is the same before and after an event within the system.

Physical laws remain the same throughout space. This means the laws of physics are the same on Earth as they are in any other part of the universe. Any point in space is equivalent to any other point in space, as far as physical laws are concerned Space is, in this sense, symmetrical.

The laws of physics also don't change with time; physical laws today are the same as they have been and will continue to be. So the laws of physics also have symmetry in time.

Noether's theorem indicates that symmetry is the fundamental reason behind the laws of conservation. For every symmetry property of a proposed theory or law, there is a corresponding conservation law; if a theory possesses certain symmetries, it implies the existence of certain important mathematical equations. The converse is also true, so if a physical quantity satisfies a conservation law, there exists a corresponding theory with appropriate symmetry that a scientist must be able to construct.

Though Noether's theorem was a mathematical development, it explained that the forces of nature arise from nature's symmetry—and in that way, it had a major implication for science in general, and theoretical physics in particular. It forms the cornerstones of work in general relativity and elementary particle physics. For example, her theorem shows that the total momentum of a system is conserved because interactions that occur don't depend upon where the system is located in space; and that it is precisely because the laws of physics don't vary with time that the total energy of a system is conserved.

Einstein's famous formula (which is often simply expressed by the equation $E=mc^2$) relates the energy, mass, and momentum of a particle. According to Noether's thorem, time is related to energy, and space is related to momentum. Because Noether's theorem shows the corresponding symmetries between time and space, and between energy and momentum, it helped to lay the mathematical foundation for the rules of quantum mechanics (the theory that predicts how subatomic particles and forces will behave).

In 1919, after World War I finally ended, the situation improved a little for German women. They were granted the

Leon Lederman *(Courtesy of U.S. Department of Energy)*

right to vote, but they were still largely prevented from teaching at institutions of higher learning; that spring, though, Emmy was allowed to complete a *"Habilitation,"* a special prerequisite for becoming a university professor in Germany.

After 1919, Noether began to concentrate on abstract algebra, a topic within the realm of pure mathematics. She became interested in ring theory. Ring theory has been described by the Nobel Laureate Leon Lederman as a mathematical theory which attempts to distill the structure of algebra down to a set of rules, by dealing with abstractions of numbers and the functions and operations that can be performed on them.

In 1921, Emmy published a paper called *"Idealtheorie in Ringbereichen,"* which was of monumental importance to the development of modern algebra. The paper provided an analysis of the fundamental structure of algebraic objects, and it also generalized an important theorem that had been proven earlier. "Noether's rings" helped to make ring theory into a major branch of mathematics. Emmy's work was changing the face of algebra.

The year was not one of undiluted success and joy, however. On December 13, 1921, Emmy's father passed away in Erlangen.

In the spring of 1922, the university finally agreed to hire Emmy as an unofficial associate professor and also gave her a teaching contract that came with a modest salary. However, this was only a partial victory. She was officially allowed to teach algebra, administer exams, and supervise dissertations. Her rights ended there. Despite her outstanding mathematical contributions, she was still denied professorship and treated as a second-class citizen: her pay was not close to the scale received by her male colleagues; nor was she granted any fringe benefits or pension rights.

Emmy refused to let the disrespectful treatment keep her from being passionate about every aspect of her work. An excellent teacher, she encouraged students to discover different ways to solve problems. Some students hated this approach and wanted clear instructions on what to do and how, but her approach attracted the most creative, gifted, and independent students. She was an animated lecturer. She usually kept a handkerchief tucked under her blouse, but while lecturing, she frequently jerked it out and thrust it back in. Before the year when she decided to crop her hair short, she wore it up in a bun, but it usually fell out of place, little by little, as her lectures progressed and Emmy moved energetically and excitedly.

Emmy was not only a scintillating teacher, she was also an unusually generous mentor. She was so giving with her students that she often planted the seeds of new and innovative ideas in their minds. Although this gave her intellectual "ownership" of much of the work that her students developed under her tutelage, she often relinquished any claim to the work in order to give them the best possible advantage as they began their careers. She was also often equally generous in providing ideas to her colleagues without enforcing her right to co-authorship of their research papers. She did, at the very least, earn a reputation for churning out talented protégés and her students were nicknamed "Noether's boys."

Emmy was as unconcerned about her own material wealth as she was about the ownership of her intellectual ideas. She hated shopping for clothes, and she usually wore a pair of thick glasses, baggy dresses, a beret, and a sturdy pair of oxford loafers because men's shoes were more comfortable to walk in. Many of her contemporaries referred to her by the masculine German article, "*der Noether*" (instead of the appropriate feminine form "*die Noether*"), partly as a joke instigated by her utter disregard for her appearance, and partly in awe of her remarkable ability to bridge the gender gap.

Emmy measured her quality of life solely by her ability to do mathematical research. Although she was incredibly daring and adventurous intellectually, her day-to-day routine was boring. It rarely wavered. She always ate at the same restaurant, at the same time, and often even ordered the same dish.

In 1924, B. L. van der Waerden, a Dutch mathematician, came to the University of Goettingen to spend a year working with Emmy. Upon his return to The Netherlands, he wrote *Moderne Algebra* (Modern Algebra), a book that discussed the latest developments in algebra. The second volume of the book was almost exclusively devoted to Emmy's work. Hermann Weyl later said that a large part of it ought really to be considered Emmy's property. Emmy's colleagues deeply respected her influence in shaping this new area of mathematical study. She revolutionized the field of modern algebra and her work led to the discovery of new algebraic patterns.

Throughout the 1920s, Emmy did groundbreaking research on various mathematical topics: abstract algebra, group theory, ring theory, group representations, and number theory. Abstract algebra extends the concepts found in elementary algebra and arithmetic into a more general realm. This branch of algebra defines and investigates algebraic structures such as groups, rings and fields. A group is a combination of a set and a single binary operation, which satisfies certain properties. Two examples of groups are: the set of integers (. . . -3, -2, 0, 1, 2, 3 . . .) under the operation of addition; and the set of rational numbers (numbers that can be expressed as the ratio of two integers) under addition. Group theory has extensive applications in mathematics, science, and engineering.

Rings are algebraic structures of a set with two particular binary operations that satisfy certain conditions, e.g. the set of all integers in which addition and multiplication are defined and follow certain properties. A field is a type of algebraic structure in which operations (such as addition and multiplication) may be performed, again obeying certain rules. Rational numbers are examples of fields. Algebraic geometry is also a part of modern algebra. It examines the algebraic aspect of geometry.

During Emmy's time, there was an intellectual debate over whether mathematics should be kept conceptual and abstract, or whether mathematics was made to be applied. Emmy's research bridged the gap between mathematical abstraction and application: her approach was abstract, but it had profound practical applications in physics and crystallography. Her work also led to a body of principles that unified different mathematical fields: algebra, geometry, linear algebra, topology, and logic. She brought about a radical change in the way that mathematicians thought, and to this day, mathematicians refer to the "Noether school" of mathematical thought.

W. Krull's *Idealtheorie*, Nathan Jacobson's *The Theory of Rings* and *Lectures in Abstract Algebra*, M. Deuring's *Algebren*, D. G. Northcott's *Ideal Theory*, and *Commutative Algebra* by Oscar Zariski and Pierre Samuel are a few basic texts exemplifying the mathematics of Emmy Noether and the school of thought she established. Emmy's mathematical genius lay in her remarkable ability to operate with abstract concepts. She did not rely or depend on concrete examples, as many did. Her vivid imagination allowed her to visualize remote connections that others missed. She constantly sought to simplify problems, and once she saw the form of a problem distinctly and clearly, she could survey the whole, relate the part back to the "big picture" overview, and integrate it into a general theory.

In 1927, Noether became an editor for the most prestigious mathematical journal of the time, *Mathematische Annalen* (the *Annals of Mathematics*). She was invited to teach a course on abstract algebra and lead a seminar on algebraic geometry at the University of Moscow during the winter of 1928. She greatly enjoyed her stay there. That year, she became the first woman to give a lecture at the prestigious International Mathematical Congress in Bologna, Italy. In 1929, she traveled

Hermann Weyl, Emmy's friend and colleague, tried to end the gender discrimination Emmy faced at the University of Goettingen. *(Courtesy of AP Images)*

to the University of Moscow as a visiting professor for the second time. One of her major contributions appeared in print that year, *Hyperkomplexe Groessen und Darstellungstheorie* (Hyper-complex sizes and representation theory).

Emmy's friend and colleague, Hermann Weyl, was promoted in 1930 to a position above Emmy's in rank. He expressed embarrassment at his promotion, because he considered Emmy to be his intellectual superior by far. Weyl did his best to work against the prevailing prejudice of the times, just as David Hilbert had done, and tried to win Emmy a promotion. That she was not even accorded equal status was another demonstration of discrimination by the German university system.

Around that time, a new type of prejudice began to infect Germany: anti-Semitism. The Nazis were seizing hold of the country. Emmy was not only of Jewish heritage, but also a feminist who sympathized with the Social Democrats, a left-wing political organization. It was only a matter of time before she came under their scrutiny.

Emmy took up an invitation to teach at the University of Frankfurt in 1930. In 1932, the International Mathematical Congress repeated this invitation to have Emmy address the group. She traveled to Zurich, Switzerland, where, of the eight hundred people attending the conference, Emmy was just one of twenty-one invited to give a major address, and the only woman invited to do so. That year, she was awarded the prestigious Alfred Ackerman-Teubner Memorial Prize for the Advancement of Mathematical Knowledge. However, Emmy was neither elected to membership in the Goettingen Association of Researchers, nor was she promoted to the rank of a full professor, because the recognition that she was starting to be showered with by her European colleagues was soon forcibly curtailed.

Early in 1933, Adolph Hitler became the official political leader of Germany. That spring he announced the beginning of his *"Third Reich."* Shortly thereafter, he passed the Enabling Act, giving himself the license to make any decree he wanted.

Adolf Hitler *(Library of Congress)*

The Nazis began to systematically dismiss people of Jewish heritage from positions of power, and oppress minority populations by committing state-sanctioned hate crimes. By April 1933, the Nazi stranglehold had tightened on German universities. Emmy received notice from the representative of the Minister for Sciences, Arts and Public Education that her right to teach was withdrawn. She was not alone. A host of other eminent mathematicians, scientists, and intellectuals who belonged to ethnic minority populations were being dismissed from the universities where they worked.

Notwithstanding this insult, Emmy continued to conduct unofficial classes in her own apartment. At one of Emmy's informal teaching sessions, a student appeared in a SS uniform, but she carried on unperturbed.

Another landmark publication of Emmy's *Nichtkommutative Algebren* (noncommutative algebra) appeared in 1933. Hermann Weyl's respect for Emmy grew even greater as he observed her behavior in the face of calamity. "I have a vivid recollection of these months . . . her courage, her frankness, her unconcern about her own fate, her conciliatory spirit . . . was, in the midst of all the hatred and meanness, despair and sorrow surrounding us, a moral solace," he wrote.

Unable to imagine the horrors that awaited them, many German Jews remained in their country, despite the blatant anti-Semitism practiced by the Nazis. Emmy was one of the lucky few who had the foresight and the opportunity to leave for safer shores. Bryn Mawr College in the United States extended an invitation to Emmy for a visiting professorship for the academic year 1933-34. Emmy also received an invitation for a professorship from Somerville College at Oxford, England. Emmy turned down the prestigious offer from Oxford and accepted the appointment at Bryn Mawr. A factor that may have influenced her decision was the presence of Anna Pell Wheeler, an American mathematician, at Bryn Mawr. Wheeler had spent some time in Goettingen, intending to write her doctoral dissertation under Emmy's colleague Hilbert.

Emmy later described her time at Bryn Mawr as the happiest in her life. She enjoyed teaching and mentoring the female undergraduates there. For the first time in her life, Emmy was surrounded by female colleagues, and that delighted her. Wheeler quickly formed a deep bond with Emmy. Unlike the German universities where Emmy had been mistreated and disgraced, "never before in her life had she received so many signs of respect, sympathy, friendship, as were bestowed upon her during her last one and a half years at Bryn Mawr."

Her visiting lectureship evolved into a regular position. Emmy joined the American Mathematical Society, and she lectured regularly at Princeton University's Institute for

Emmy accepted an invitation to teach at Bryn Mawr College in Pennsylvania to escape the Jewish persecution in Germany. *(Courtesy of Andre Jenny/Alamy)*

Advanced Study, where two of her admiring male colleagues, Albert Einstein and Hermann Weyl, had sought refuge after fleeing Germany. Emmy was appreciated in Bryn Mawr and Princeton as she never had been in her own country.

In the summer of 1934, Emmy returned briefly to the University of Goettingen. She was shocked to find that even in the once-cloistered university environment, conditions had taken a dramatic turn for the worse. Many of her former friends and colleagues ignored her. Though Emmy "harbored no grudge against Goettingen and her fatherland for what they had done to her," she decided to immigrate to the United States. She shipped her meager belongings to Pennsylvania and took leave of her friends and family.

Emmy's American women students welcomed her return; but although "her girl students here were as near to her heart as the Noether boys had been in Goettingen," Emmy was unfortunately unable to develop their talents to the same extent as she had done with her male European students, not because she had lost her passion for mentoring, but because her life was already approaching its end. At the age of fifty-three, just two years after joining the college, she was diagnosed with an ovarian tumor. Emmy hid the bad news about her health from all but those she was closest to. As she suffered from high blood pressure, it was risky for her to have surgery, but the tumor had to be removed. Early in April of 1935, Emmy underwent surgery. Four days later, she developed post-operative complications. Her temperature rose to 109 degrees and she lapsed into a coma. Doctors were uncertain of why this had happened, and thought she may have succumbed to an unidentified post-surgical viral infection.

Emmy did not recover. On April 14, 1935, Emmy succumbed to a stroke. Her untimely death was a shock to most of those around her. Her friend Hermann Weyl, in his memorial address delivered in Goodhart Hall at Bryn Mawr College, on April 26, 1935, compared her favorably to Sonya Kovalevskaya in terms of the two womens' mathematical abilities as well as their personalities. He said:

> Emmy Noether without doubt possessed by far the greater power, the greater scientific talent . . . Indeed, two traits determined above all her nature: first, the native productive power of her mathematical genius. She was not clay, pressed by the artistic hands of God into a harmonious form, but rather a chunk of human primary rock into which he had blown his creative breath of life. Second, her heart knew no malice; she did not believe in evil—indeed it never entered her mind that it could play a role among men. This was never more forcefully apparent to me than in the last stormy summer, that of 1933, which we spent together in Goettingen. The memory of her work in science and

of her personality among her fellows will not soon pass away. She was a great mathematician, the greatest, I firmly believe that her sex has ever produced, and a great woman.

By then, Emmy's contributions were legendary. She was widely respected by mathematicians and physicists for laying the foundation of new fields of algebraic study, and the proof of two theorems (one of which bore her name) that were basic for both general relativity and elementary particle physics.

Obituaries began to pour in, written in several different languages—a testament to the global significance of Emmy's work. In an obituary that appeared in *Mathematische Annalen*, the journal on whose editorial board Emmy had served, B. L. van der Waerden wrote that "her originality" was "absolute beyond comparison . . . it lay in the fundamental structure of her creative mind, in the mode of her thinking and in the aim of her endeavors."

Albert Einsten wrote a tribute to her that was published in the *New York Times* the May after the year of her death: "In the judgment of the most competent living mathematicians, Fraeulein Noether was the most significant creative mathematical genius thus far produced since the higher education of women began. In the realm of algebra, in which the most gifted mathematicians have been busy for centuries, [she] discovered methods which have proved of enormous importance."

Posthumous accolades rolled in many years after Emmy's death in the country of her birth. In 1958, on the fiftieth anniversary of Emmy's receipt of her doctoral degree, the University of Erlangen, which had never provided Emmy with monetary compensation for her research and teaching, nevertheless invited many of "Noether's boys" for a reunion to celebrate and discuss Emmy's impact on mathematics. In 1960, the city of Erlangen named a street *Noetherstrasse* [Noether's Street] in her honor. The Mathematical Institute at University of Erlangen unveiled a memorial tablet in her honor in 1982. On the hundredth anniversary of her birth, in 1993, the city of Erlangen dedicated a newly constructed school to her, the Emmy Noether Gymnasium.

On the centenary of her birth, the American Mathematical Society held a conference at Bryn Mawr to honor her. In the words of her longtime friend Hermann Weyl, "It shall not be forgotten what America did during these last two stress-ful years for Emmy Noether and for German science in general."

timeline

1882	Born in Erlangen, Germany, on March 23.
1900	One of two women students allowed to attend lectures at the University of Erlangen.
1907	Completes doctoral thesis.
1908-	
1915	Works without pay at the Mathematical Institute in Erlangen.
1916	Moves to Goettingen but despite six published

mathematical research papers, is refused a paid position because of gender.

1919   Given unofficial professorship by University of Goettingen.

1925   Completes manuscript *"Abstrackter Augbau der Idealtheorie in Zahl und Funktronenkoerpern."*

1928   Invited to address the International Congress of Mathematics.

1928-
1929   Accepts invitation to travel to Moscow as visiting professor.

1930   Accepts invitation to act as visiting professor at Frankfurt.

1932   Completes the manuscript *"Nichtkommutative Algebren;"* awarded the Alfred Ackerman Teubner Memorial Prize for the advancement of mathematical sciences.

1933   Right to teach withdrawn by Nazi ordinance; leaves Germany for the United States to teach at Bryn Mawr.

1935   Dies at the age of fifty-three as a result of post-surgical complications arising after the removal of a tumor; leaves behind forty-four important mathematical publications.

Sources

CHAPTER ONE: Emilie de Breteuil

p. 18, "The fruit of your . . .," David Bodanis, *Passionate Minds: The Great Enlightenment Love Affair* (London: Little, Brown, 2006), 95.

p. 22, "Its author is a young . . ." Ibid., 126.

p. 25, "I shall await you . . ." Ibid., 234.

CHAPTER TWO: Maria Gaetana Agnesi

p. 27, "It will perhaps seem . . ." Rebecca Messbarger and Paula Findlen, eds, *Maria Gaetana Agnesi et alia. The Contest For Knowledge* (Chicago: University of Chicago Press, 2005), 129.

p. 28, "weaken and destroy . . ." Ibid., 130.

p. 28, "content with the management . . ." Ibid.

p. 28, "bathe the tender minds . . ." Ibid., 137.

p. 28, "the eternal drought of ignorance," Ibid.

p. 28, "Thus, I ask this one last thing . . ." Ibid., 139-140.

CHAPTER THREE: Mary Somerville

p. 42, "a small quiet seaport . . ." Mary Somerville, *Personal Recollections from Early Life to Old Age of Mary Somerville, with Selections from her Correspondence* (Boston: Roberts Brothers, 1873), 10.

p. 42, "My mother taught me . . ." Ibid., 17.

p. 42, "which flourished luxuriantly on . . ." Ibid., 11.

p. 42-43, "knew most of them . . ." Ibid., 18.

p. 43, "was between eight and . . ." Ibid., 20-21.

p. 43, "all that a woman . . ." Ibid., 25.

p. 43, "The chief thing I had . . ." Ibid., 22.

p. 44, "a wild animal escaped . . ." Ibid., 20.

p. 44, "watched the crabs . . ." Ibid., 26.

p. 44, "small collection of books . . ." Ibid., 27.

p. 44-45, "turn for reading . . ." Ibid., 28.

p. 45, "spent many hours . . ." Ibid., 30.

p. 46, "on the contrary . . ." Ibid., 37.

p. 46, "I never was happier . . ." Ibid.

p. 46, "Though kind in the main . . ." Ibid., 42.

p. 47, "made considerable progress . . ." Ibid., 43.

p. 47, "could remember neither . . ." Ibid., 29.

p. 47, "The Liberals were . . ." Ibid., 45-46.

p. 48, "Strange to say, she . . ." Ibid., 46.

p. 48, "At the end of a page . . ." Ibid.

p. 48, "I never lost sight . . ." Ibid., 50.

p. 49, "took a fancy to . . ." Ibid., 48.

p. 49, "to get elementary books . . ." Ibid.

p. 49, "You should study Euclid's . . ." Ibid., 49.

p. 50, "'It was no wonder . . ." Ibid., 54.

p. 50, "already gone through . . ." Ibid.

p. 51, "fond of dancing . . ." Ibid., 63.

p. 51, "Had it been my . . ." Ibid., 59-60.

p. 51, "I was alone the . . ." Ibid., 75.

p. 52-53, "told him that I . . ." Ibid., 79.

p. 53, "I could hardly believe . . ." Ibid., 79-80.

p. 54, "foolish manner of life . . ." Ibid., 88.

p. 54, "still more so. . ." Ibid.

p. 54, "my cookery was needed . . ." Ibid., 89.

p. 56, "I never was so . . ." Ibid., 153.

p. 59, "self-acquired knowledge . . ." Ibid., 162-163.

p. 60, "astonished at the success . . ." Ibid., 173.

p. 60, "When Mrs. Somerville shows . . ." Ibid., 171.

p. 60, "considered it to be . . ." Ibid., 172.

p. 60, "with the highest admiration . . ." Ibid., 167.

p. 62, "the warmth with which . . ." Ibid., 176.

p. 65, "We English cannot . . ." Ibid., 363-364.

p. 66, "I am now in . . ." Ibid., 364.

p. 66, "She always retained . . ." Ibid., 376-377.

CHAPTER FOUR: Ada Byron Lovelace

p. 75-76, "I shall be very grateful . . ." Betty A. Toole, ed., *Ada, The Enchantress of Numbers: A Selection from the Letters of Lord Byron's Daughter and her Description of the First Computer* (Mill Valley, CA: Strawberry Press, 1992), 54.

p. 84, "does not occupy common . . ." Ada Byron Lovelace, "Sketch of the Analytic Engine," Taylor's Scientific Memoirs, http://www.fourmilab.ch/babbage/sketch.html.

p. 84, "We may say most . . ." Ibid.

p. 84, "equally capable of analysis . . ." Ibid.

p. 85, "Supposing, for instance . . ." Ibid.

p. 85, "might compose elaborate . . ." Ibid.

p. 86, "The further we . . ." Ibid.

p. 86, "a method was devised . . ." Ibid.

p. 87, "whenever a general term . . ." Ibid.

p. 88, "The Analytical Engine has . . ." Ibid.

p. 88, "indirect and reciprocal . . ." Ibid.

p. 89, "the Deborah, the Elijah . . ." Toole, *Ada, The Enchantress of Numbers,* 291.

p. 90, "Prophetess . . . Integral!" Ibid., 292 .

CHAPTER FIVE: Sonya Kovalevsky

p. 96, "on ordinary occasions . . ." Sonya Kovalevsky, *Sonya Kovalevsky: Her Recollections of Childhood* (New York: The Century Co., 1895), 46.

p. 97, "a spacious, but low-ceilinged . . ." Ibid., 3.

p. 97, "A chiming of bells . . ." Ibid., 2.

p. 97, "very handsome woman . . ." Ibid., 4.

p. 97, "or tearing her gown . . . corner with shame." Ibid., 7.

p. 97, "the master and mistress . . ." Ibid., 10.

p. 98, "suddenly made the unexpected . . ." Ibid., 35.

p. 98, "The tutor was a quiet . . ." Ibid., 36.

p. 98, "the center and goal . . ." Ibid., 50.

p. 98, "through all the memories . . ." Ibid.

p. 98, "for a strong and exclusive affection . . ." Ibid., 53.

p. 98, "governess did not approve . . ." Ibid., 43.

p. 98, "the very rhythm . . . " Ibid.

p. 98, "passionately fond . . ." Ibid.

p. 98, "was destined to become . . ." Ibid., 44.

p. 99, "in a chronic state . . ." Ibid., 45.

p. 99, "admired her beyond measure . . ." Ibid., 78.

p. 99, "shouted at her . . ." Ibid., 99.

p. 99, "became watchful . . ." Ibid., 100.

p. 99, "felt instinctively that Aniuta . . ." Ibid., 101.

p. 99, "after one particularly stormy scene . . ." Ibid., 101.

p. 100, "From the top of . . ." Ibid., 120.

p. 101, "A feeling of reckless . . ." Ibid., 151.

p. 101, "particularly strong attachments," Ibid., 53.

p. 101, "scientific lectures," Ibid., 72.

p. 101, "library was his favorite nook," Ibid., 54.

p. 101, "was carried away . . ." Ibid., 55.

p. 101, "together for hours at . . ." Ibid., 65.

p. 102, "Although he had never . . ." Ibid., 65.

p. 102, "a reverence for mathematics . . ." Ibid., 65.

p. 102, "first encounters with . . ." Ibid., 66.

p. 102, "by a happy accident," Sonya Kovalevsky, *A Russian Childhood* (New York: Springer-Verlag, 1978), 215.

p. 102, "speckled over with some . . ." Ibid.

p. 102, "would stand by the . . ." Ibid.

p. 102, "As a result of my . . . " Ibid.

p. 102, "The depth of that . . ." Ibid.

p. 102, "was taking lessons from . . ." Ibid.

p. 102, "first systematic study . . ." Ibid.

p. 102, "dim recollection," Ibid.

p. 102, "there is no question . . ." Ibid.

p. 103, "much more taken . . ." Ibid.

p. 103, "the philosophical aspect . . ." Ibid.

p. 103, "an attraction to mathematics . . ." Ibid.

p. 103, "who in any case . . ." Ibid.

p. 103, "to wheedle out of . . ." Ibid., 217.

p. 103, "chagrin . . . encountered trigonometric . . ." Ibid.

p. 103, "he replied that he . . ." Ibid.

p. 103, "the same road . . ." Ibid.

p. 104, "He went straight to . . ." Ibid., 218.

p. 106, "one of the greatest . . ." Ibid., 219.

p. 108, "completed three: two in . . ." Ibid.

p. 109, "Except for correcting . . ." Pelegeya Kochina, *Love and Mathematics: Sofya Kovalevskaya* (Moscow: Mir Publishers, 1985) 82.

p. 109, "This honor, given to . . . Kovalevsky, *A Russian Childhood*, 219.

p. 110, "most gifted of the . . ." Ibid., 221.

p. 111, "you won't believe how . . ." Kochina, *Love and Mathematics*, 51-52.

p. 111, "far less zealously than . . ." Kovalevsky, *A Russian Childhood*, 220.

p. 111, "some feeling of scholarly . . ." Ibid.

p. 112, "At that time all . . ." Ibid.

p. 112-113, "I was twenty-two years . . ." Sonya Kovalevsky, *Nihilist Girl* (New York: Modern Language Association of America, 2001), 3.

p. 113, "I am even not . . ." Kochina, *Love and Mathematics*, 93.

p. 116, "my work was completed . . ." Kovalevsky, *A Russian Childhood*, 221.

p. 117, "Gave the first lecture . . ." Kochina, *Love and Mathematics*, 131.

p. 118, "The problem, which encompasses . . ." Kovalevsky, *A Russian Childhood*, 226.

p. 120, "was found deserving . . ." Ibid., 227.

p. 120, "was given a highly ceremonial . . ." Ibid.

CHAPTER SIX: Emmy Noether

p. 130, *"Das ist nicht Mathematik; das ist Theologie,"* James W. Brewer, Martha K. Smith, and Emmy Noether, eds., *Emmy Noether: A Tribute to her Life and Work* (New York: Dekker, 1981), 11.

p. 130, *"rechnerei . . . formelngestruepp,"* Auguste Dick, *Emmy Noether, 1882-1935,* trans. H. I. Blocher (Boston: Birkhauser, 1981), 155.

p. 130, *"Hilbert will naechste Woch . . ."* Dick, *Emmy Noether*, 12.

p. 131, "Yesterday, I received . . ." Ibid., 13.

p. 141-142, "I have a vivid recollection . . ." Ibid., 132.

p. 142, "never before in her life . . ." Ibid., 133.

p. 143, "harbored no grudge . . ." Ibid.

p. 143, "her girl students . . ." Ibid.

p. 144, "Emmy Noether without doubt . . ." Ibid., 151-152.

p. 145, "her originality . . . her endeavors," Ibid., 100.

p. 145, "In the judgment of . . ." Albert Einstein, "Letter to the *New York Times*, May 5, 1935," reprinted in Dick, 92-94.

p. 146, "It shall not be forgotten . . ." Dick, *Emily Noether*, 134.

Bibliography

Baum, Joan. *The Calculating Passion of Ada Byron.*
Hamden, CT: Archon Books, 1986.

Bell, E. T. *Master and Pupil: Weierstrass (1815-1897) and
Sonja Kowalewski (1850-1891).* New York: Simon
and Schuster, 1986.

———. *Men of Mathematics: The Lives and Achievements
of the Great Mathematicians from Zeno to Poincare.*
New York: Simon and Schuster, 1986.

Bodanis, David. *Passionate Minds: The Great Enlightenment
Love Affair.* London: Little, Brown, 2006.

Bohn, Marcia. *Emmy Noether, A Woman of Greatness.*
AuthorHouse, 2005.

Bölling, Reinhard. *Deine* "Sonia: A reading from a burned
letter," *The Mathematical Intelligencer* 14, no.3, (1992).

Brewer, James, and Martha K. Smith, eds. *Emmy Noether,
A Tribute to her Life and Work.* New York: Marcel
Dekker, 1981.

Cooke, Roger. *The Mathematics of Sonya Kovalevskaya.*
New York: Springer-Verlag, 1984.

———. "S.V. Kovalevskaya's Mathematical Legacy: The
Rotation of a Rigid Body." In *Vita Mathematica:
Historical Research and Integration with Teaching*,
by Ronald Calinger. Washington, DC: Mathematical
Association of America, 1996.

Dick, Auguste. *Emmy Noether, 1882-1935.* Translated by
H. I. Blocher. Boston: Birkhauser, 1981.

Durant, Will, and Ariel Durant. *The Age of Voltaire.* New
York: Simon and Schuster, 1965.

Einstein, Albert. "Letter to the New York Times, May 5,
1935." *New York Times.*

Grinstein Louise S., and P. J. Campbell. *Women of
Mathematics: A Bio-bibliographic Sourcebook.* New
York: Greenwood Press, 1987.

Keen, L. "The Legacy of Sonya Kovalevskaya." Proceedings
of a symposium sponsored by the Association for Women

in Mathematicis and the Mary Ingraham Buntin Institute, American Mathematical Society, Providence, 1986.

Kennedy, D. H. *Little Sparrow: A Portrait of Sophia Kovalevsky.* Ohio: Ohio University Press, 1983.

Kleiner, I. "Emmy Noether: Highlights of her life and work," *L'Ensignement Mathématique* 38 (1992).

Koblitz, A. H. *A Convergence of Lives: Sofia Kovalevskaia: Scientist, Writer, Revolutionary.* Boston: Birkhaeuser, 1983.

Koblitz, A. H. "Sofia Kovalevskaia and the Mathematical Community." *The Mathematical Intelligencer* 6 (1984): 20-29.

Kochina, Pelegeya. *Love and Mathematics: Sofya Kovalevskaya.* Translated by Michael Burov. Moscow: Mir Publishers, 1985.

Kovalevsky, Sonya. *A Russian Childhood.* Translated and edited by Beatrice Stillman. New York: Springer-Verlag, 1978.

Kovalevsky, Sonya. *Nihilist Girl.* New York: Modern Language Association of America, 2001.

Kovalevsky, Sonya. *Sonya Kovalevsky: Her Recollections of Childhood.* Translated by Isabel F. Hapgood. New York: The Century Co., 1895.

Kovalevsky, Sonya, and A. C. Leffler. *Biography and Autobiography.* Translated by Louise von Cossel. New York: MacMillan, 1895.

Lanczos, Cornelius. "Emmy Noether and the calculus of variations." *Bulletin of the Institute of Mathematics and its Applications* 9, no. 8: (1973): 253-258.

Lederman, L., and C. T. Hill, *Symmetry and the Beautiful Universe.* New York: Prometheus Books, 2004.

Messbarger, Rebecca, and P. Findlen, eds. and trans. *The Contest for Knowledge Debates Over Women's learning in the Eighteenth-Century Italy.* Chicago: University of Chicago Press, 2005.

Moore, Doris Langley. *Ada Countess of Lovelace: Byron's*

Legitimate Daughter. New York: Harper and Row publishers, 1977.

Mozans, H. J. *Woman in Science*. Notre Dame, Indiana: University of Notre Dame Press, 1991.

Neely, K. A. *Mary Somerville: Science, Illumination and the Female Mind*. Cambridge: Cambridge University Press, 2001.

Osen, L. M. *Women in Mathematics*. Cambridge, MA: MIT Press, 1974.

Patterson, E. C. *Mary Somerville and the Cultivation of Science, 1815-1840*. The Hague: Martinus Nijhoff Publishers, 1983.

Perl, T. H. *Math Equals: Biographies of Women Mathematicians + Related Activities*. Menlo Park, CA: Addison-Wesley Publishing Company, 1978.

Rappaport, K. "S Kovalevsky: A Mathematical Lesson." *American Mathematical Monthly* 88, no. 8 (1981): 564-574.

Smith, D. E. *History of Mathematics*. New York: Dover Publications, 1951.

Somerville, Mary. *Personal Recollections from Early Life to Old Age of Mary Somerville, with Selections from her Correspondence*. Boston: Roberts Brothers, 1873.

Spicci, J. *Beyond the Limit: The Dream of Sofya Kovalevskaya*. New York: Tom Doherty Associates, LLC, 2002.

Toole, B. A., ed. *Ada, the enchantress of Numbers: A selection from the letters of Lord Byron's daughter and her description of the first computer*. Mill Valley, CA: Strawberry Press, 1992.

van der Waerden, B. L. *History of Algebra*. Berlin: Springer-Verlag, 1985.

Wade, Mary Dodson. *Ada Byron Lovelace: the lady and the computer*. New York: Macmillan Publishing Company, 1994.

Weyl, Hermann. "Emmy Noether," *Scripta mathematica* 3, (1935).

Web sites

http://www.awm-math.org/biographies.html
The Association for Women in Mathematics maintains this site, which features profiles of dozens of women mathematicians as well as scientists.

http://www.agnesscott.edu/lriddle/women/alpha.htm
Thanks to Agnes Scott College, a private liberal arts college in Atlanta, Georgia, this Web site provides visitors with an alphabetical listing of women in the field of mathematics, from ancient to modern time. Each woman's achievements are highlighted in a biographical sketch, accompanied by reference material.

http://www.sdsc.edu/ScienceWomen/noether.html
Emmy Noether and Ada Byron are two of sixteen women scientists profiled in the "Women in Science" online publication sponsored by the San Diego Supercomputer Center.

http://www-groups.dcs.st-and.ac.uk/~history/Indexes/Women.html
Biographies of female mathematicians from various centuries and countries are featured on the MacTutor History of Mathematics archive, maintained by the School of Mathematics and Statistics at the University of St. Andrews, Scotland.

Index